ARY

Understanding Culture

Understanding Culture

cultural studies, order, ordering

Gavin Kendall

and

Gary Wickham

SAGE Publications
London • Thousand Oaks • New Delhi

SAGE Publications Ltd
6 Bonhill Street
London EC2A 4PU

SAGE Publications Inc.
2455 Teller Road
Thousand Oaks, California 91320

SAGE Publications India Pvt Ltd
32, M-Block Market
Greater Kailash – I
New Delhi 110 048

British Library Cataloguing in Publication data

A catalogue record for this book is
available from the British Library

ISBN 0 7619 6514 9
ISBN 0 7619 6515 7 (pbk)

Library of Congress control number available

Typeset by M Rules
Printed in Great Britain by Biddles, Guildford, Surrey

Contents

Acknowledgements

Among the many people – friends, family and colleagues – to whom we have become indebted while writing this book, we should especially like to thank the following: Eric Bredo, Alan Collins, Susan Condor, Jo Goodie, Jeremy Kendall, Kate Kendall, Trisha Kendall, Jeff Malpas, Mike Michael, Katherine Sheehan, and David Silverman. Thanks are also owed to the staff at Sage, whose encouragement and professionalism made our task so much easier and so much more enjoyable. An earlier version of some of the ideas in Chapter 4 appeared in the *Australian Journal of Political Science* (1997) 32(2): 223–35, under the title 'Governing at a distance'. Chapter 7 represents work, some of which has been and is being conducted with Mike Michael; it has been impossible entirely to disentangle Mike's contribution, but he bears no responsibility for any errors in the chapter or problems with the argument.

Introduction: Cultural Studies with Just a Hint of Foucault

Yes, this is another Cultural Studies book influenced by Michel Foucault, but he does not block the sun. He may pop his head up occasionally in the following pages, and his ghost trips across our words, no doubt about it, but Foucault here is, in the main, a quiet background figure. We suggest this 'quiet background' Foucaultian influence on our book has three aspects.

First, we owe a debt to some existing books that use Foucault in one way or another to address, at least in some respects, the ground of the discipline, or disciplines, or inter- or intra- or anti-disciplinary groupings, known as Cultural Studies. The debt is more and less direct, but however direct, we have benefited from the ways in which the following books make use of Foucault's thinking: Ian Hunter's *Culture and Government* (1988), Tony Bennett's *Culture: A Reformer's Science* (1998), Alec McHoul and Toby Miller's *Popular Culture and Everyday Life* (1998) and Tom Osborne's *Aspects of Enlightenment* (1998). The following formulation by Osborne captures the way in which Foucault finds his way into Osborne's book, into the other books mentioned, and into the one (we hope) you are about to read:

> [T]he Foucault that makes an appearance is not perhaps the usual, erstwhile trendy one. The sort of Foucault that appeals to me is not, anyway, the Foucault that appears in the cribs; the subversive continental philosopher, the arcane prophet of transgression, the iconoclastic poststructuralist, the meta-theorist of power, the functionalist theorist of social control, or the gloomy prophet of the totally administered society. These sorts of Foucault can all safely be forgotten. The Foucault that motivates much of this book – more often than not behind the scenes – is a much more buttoned-up animal . . . a good modernist rather than a faddish postmodernist, a rigorous and not so unconventional historical epistemologist. . . . This, then, is

> not the naughty, transgressive Foucault, but rather – as I once heard it described – Foucault with his clothes on. (1998: x)

Second, we are pointedly Foucaultian in the way we set out to disturb any obviousness Cultural Studies might have gathered about itself. If you were even in the least bit surprised by our awkward qualification of this term employed immediately above – the discipline, or disciplines, or inter- or intra- or anti-disciplinary groupings, known as Cultural Studies – then maybe you've become too settled about Cultural Studies, too accepting of what the dominant version of it has to say about itself.

This is to say we are involved here in polemic. We do not like this dominant version, with its obsession with power-and-meanings, to be described in our first chapter. We aim to challenge its dominance. We do not like the fact that it seems to have lost sight of the complexity of its central notion, culture – even in the 1951 *Encyclopaedia of the Social Sciences* there were 78 definitions of 'culture', which alone should be enough to keep the contentious and elusive character of this notion in the foreground. And we do not like the fact that it seems to have lost sight of its own twisted history. As we demonstrate in the first chapter, Cultural Studies has been and can be anything from the study of agriculture, to the study of 'high' culture, the study of 'low' culture, the study of the cultures of 'other', exotic lands, and the study of the culture of our selves (among others).

Third, in proposing a direction that is more aware of the complexities of culture and more aware of the complex history of Cultural Studies, we propose Cultural Studies as the study of ordering. Chapter 2 spells out in detail what we mean by ordering, but it will not spoil the story if we tell you that our thinking about ordering is built on an understanding of order, that is built on an understanding of governance, that is built on an understanding of Foucault's notion of governmentality. However, we do not say anything directly about 'governmentality' in this book, so, just in case you are not familiar with the body of work that has emerged around this neologism of Foucault – often called 'the governmentality approach' – here are a couple of useful quotations to help situate it. The first comes from Pat O'Malley:

> There is a considerable literature exploring and developing this approach. . . . Such work has been influenced strongly by the thinking of Michel Foucault . . . but has been advanced primarily in recent years by British and Australian scholars. The journal *Economy and Society* has been

a principal site for the development of this approach, which is frequently referred to as the 'governmentality' literature. While 'governmentality' refers to a particular technology of government that emerges in the eighteenth century, the term is more generally used to refer to the approach adopted in its study. The approach is characterised by two primary characteristics. The first is a stress on the dispersal of 'government', that is, on the idea that government is not a preserve of 'the state' but is carried out at all levels and sites in societies – including the self government of individuals. . . . The second is the deployment of an analytic stance that favours 'how' questions over 'why' questions. In other words it favours accounts in terms of how government of a certain kind becomes possible: in what manner it is thought up by planners, using what concepts; how it is intended to be translated into practice, using what combination of means? Only secondarily is it concerned with accounts that seek to explain government – in the sense of understanding the nature of government as the effect of other events. (1998–9: 679 n. 7)

The second quotation is from Mitchell Dean:

It is possible to distinguish two broad meanings of this term in the literature. The second is a historically specific version of the first. . . . In this first sense, the term 'governmentality' suggests what we have just noted. It deals with how we think about governing, with the different mentalities of government. . . . The notions of collective mentalities and the idea of a history of mentalities have long been used by sociologists (such as Emile Durkheim and Marcel Mauss) and by the *Annales* school of history in France. . . . For such thinkers, a mentality is a collective, relatively bounded unity, and is not readily examined by those who inhabit it. . . . The idea of mentalities of government, then, emphasizes the way in which the thought involved in practices of government is collective and relatively taken for granted. . . . [This] is to say that the way we think about exercising authority draws upon the theories, ideas, philosophies and forms of knowledge that are part of our social and cultural products. (1999: 16)

This discussion has served to introduce the content of Chapters 1 and 2 – a survey of the field of Cultural Studies in which we do not hide our disquiet about the way it has developed (Chapter 1) and an excursion into the notion of ordering as a possible means of organising Cultural Studies (Chapter 2). Chapter 3 sets out a method to allow Cultural Studies to be the study of ordering without it lapsing into the bad habits that, we argue have dogged the field for too long; we rely on a combination of Wittgenstein and some ancient philosophy to get this job done (Foucault remaining, as we assured you he does, in the background). The other four chapters lay our vision before you in all its glory (or otherwise): a chance for you to see what Cultural Studies as the study of ordering might look like. Chapter 4 deals with the culture of colonial government and Chapter 5 with the culture of law and regulation. In these two chapters we thereby subtly attempt to expand the horizons of Cultural Studies. Chapters 6 and 7 are much more within the usual Cultural Studies territory, although we hope they look sufficiently awkward and strange to a traditional Cultural Studies eye. In Chapter 6 we examine the culture of the everyday and in Chapter 7 'identity' and the construction of the self through technical and technological routinisation.

1 Surveying the Field of Cultural Studies

We feel compelled to warn you. This chapter is not about Cultural Studies as we think it should be, but about Cultural Studies as it has been and is practised. We give only some hints here about the way we think it should be – something that fills the other chapters. But, it has to be acknowledged, our disquiet about the way it has been and is practised will hit you well before you reach the other chapters (it already has). We try to limit our expressions of disquiet to those necessary to establish that Cultural Studies is in poor health – enough to need our doctoring – but it might well be that we are not as circumspect as we think we are.

Early Cultural Studies (and here we are thinking particularly about British Cultural Studies as it emerged in the 1950s) prided itself on its inter-disciplinary, even anti-disciplinary nature: Cultural Studies drew strength from the fact that it was not the slave of any singular disciplinary thought. Cultural Studies located itself as always more than a 'mere' academic discipline, seeing itself engaging in the analysis of power without disciplinary constraint. Cultural Studies, then, saw itself as waging a kind of guerrilla war against 'the disciplines', inasmuch as the latter were seen as props for the maintenance of an iniquitous social order (it has to be added that Cultural Studies knew 'the disciplines' not in their specificity, but as a general enemy). With this set of moves, Cultural Studies ensured that 'culture' was never a simple, given object of inquiry. The emphasis on power meant that Cultural Studies was always 'strategic' in what it examined, and consequently the decision about what counted as 'culture' was a shifting and complex problem. It has to be added that for many of its adherents the past tense is inappropriate – this is still what Cultural Studies is like for many.

Of course, we stereotype here. Nonetheless, we are sure our some-what crude portrayal offered so far is very near the mark. We take most of the chapter to show that it is.

We begin the main work of the chapter with a brief tour though the history of the use of the term 'culture' and the corresponding term 'Cultural Studies'. We then look at the important roles played by anthropology and sociology in defining 'culture'. We extend this by considering Cultural Studies as a sort of 'anthropology of home', and it is in this section that we describe the birth of the modern discipline of Cultural Studies in Britain. This takes us into a section in which we discuss more directly the political obsessions of British Cultural Studies. Following this, we discuss the development of Cultural Studies through its engagement with continental European thought (we nominate Gramsci, Foucault and de Certeau as Cultural Studies' most important figures). Finally, we sketch at least some of the ways in which Cultural Studies has become even more heterogeneous through its implantation and adaptation in the United States, Australia and elsewhere.

Raymond Williams: from 'agriculture' to 'culture'

Raymond Williams's (1983) *Keywords* helps us understand Cultural Studies' uses of the term 'culture', as well as the origins of its distinction between high and low culture. First, Williams mentions how the original meaning of 'culture' was linked to the tending of crops and animals – as in agriculture (Williams 1983: 87). By the time of the Enlightenment, 'culture' was being used as a synonym for 'civilisation'. Culture, then, came to represent a path of progress (progress leading to the European civilisations), and was typically used in the singular. In the nineteenth century, in a move which Williams especially associates with Herder and the German Romantics, as well as with the rise of nationalism, 'culture' came to be associated with different and specific ways of life, particularly those that could be seen in the different nations of the world and in the different regions of those nations. Thus, 'cultures' could be comfortably used as a plural. By the second half of the nineteenth century (and here Williams mentions specifically the influence of Matthew Arnold's *Culture and Anarchy*, 1932, first published in 1869), the pluralised 'cultures' were now understood by being broken into better and worse types of culture (and, revealingly, Arnold is famous for his popularisation of the word 'philistine'), so much so that the term 'culture' became associated with the 'high arts' – philosophy and the other liberal arts, classical music and literature, painting, sculpture, and so forth.

At the turn of the twentieth century, in tandem with the emergence of the human and social sciences (especially anthropology and sociology), culture became most closely associated with meaning. Williams terms this the *social* definition of culture, and it is worth quoting him on this point. Offering a 'social definition of culture', he says:

> Culture is a description of a particular way of life which expresses certain meanings and values not only in art and learning but also in institutions and ordinary behaviour. The analysis of culture, from such a definition, is the clarification of the meanings and values implicit and explicit in particular ways of life, a particular 'culture'. (1961: 57)

We see here one of the early expressions of a particularly enduring theme of this type of Cultural Studies: the idea that culture is all around us. Elsewhere, Williams (1958) famously titles and begins a seminal essay with the three-word catchphrase 'culture is ordinary'.

Anthropology and sociology as studies of culture

Williams claims there is no real difference between studying 'culture' and studying 'society'. In making this equivalence, he is indebted to Émile Durkheim's notion of the 'conscience collective', those collective representations which bind society together – the shared understandings, values, norms and beliefs that people hold as they go about their mundane existence. For Durkheim, these collective beliefs were social in origin, but typically worked at the level of the individual, giving each of us a way to understand what is good, what is evil, what is moral, what is immoral, and so forth. In a sense, what Durkheim tried to do was a kind of anthropology of home – an inquiry into the systems of thought that held our society together, equivalent to the anthropologists' studies of the systems of thought that were the glue for exotic and strange societies.

E.B. Tylor, the nineteenth-century British anthropologist, defined culture in evolutionary terms (see especially Tylor 1871); Margaret Mead, the American anthropologist defined culture as a learned phenomenon (see especially Mead 1964, 1976); Clifford Geertz informed us that culture is relative, nothing special, and the result of local storytelling (see especially Geertz 1991, 2000). These anthropological definitions are a useful starting point in our quest to understand Cultural Studies. From Tylor's evolutionism to Mead's behaviourism to Geertz's relativism, we see some of the main themes that have dominated anthropological Cultural Studies. What is still retained today in the field is a commitment to relativism and behaviourism (that is to say, all cultures are equal, strange, learned and unnatural). To a certain extent, Tylor's Whiggish ethnocentrism has bitten the dust.

Anthropology emerged in Europe over the course of the nineteenth century, a gradual, and in its origins profoundly amateur, project. By 1884 it had really arrived as an academic discipline, with the foundation of the first university post in anthropology (at Oxford for Tylor) and by being given its own section (Section H) within the British Association for the Advancement of Science. Tylor's evolutionist theory of culture stressed gradual steady development, based on human creativity. Small innovations by outstanding individuals allowed a culture to improve, but in thinking about the timescale for these developments Tylor followed Darwin's emphasis in the field of evolution, and suggested that changes in a culture were virtually imperceptible because they happened over such an extended time period. However, unlike Darwin, Tylor believed that cultural evolution was always oriented toward increasing civilisation, and consequently progress was inevitable (and relatively easily achievable should a civilised culture need to step in to remedy the problems of a pathological savage society). Tylor developed a three-stage evolutionism, with societies starting at savagery, moving through barbarism and eventually reaching civilisation (see critical discussions of this theory in Kuklick 1991; Stocking 1982, 1992). 'Culture', then, was broadly equated with a society's habits, beliefs, and so forth, but some cultures were better than others. For Tylor, civilised Western societies were the pinnacle of achievement and the first-ranked of all possible societies (see also Frazer 1890; Morgan 1877, 1876/1997).

This conceptualisation of culture had some important consequences for our fledgling Cultural Studies: anthropology, like all the nineteenth-century human sciences, became intimately linked to programmes of social management, providing an intellectual proving-ground for colonialist attempts to revive or inject culture into foreign countries. The model from evolution (and we are aware that this model was a simplified and erroneous model) was so seductive that analogous arguments about the progress of culture were made in a variety of academic and governmental problem areas: just as the West could claim to be culturally superior to the rest of the world, so it was thought that similar processes could be uncovered to explain the cultural superiority of men over women, whites over blacks, rich over poor, law-abiders over criminals.

The signs of this cultural superiority were written on the bodies of our nascent human sciences' objects of study. For example, Cesare Lombroso famously developed his criminology based on the idea that the criminal was atavistic, and, in a rather circular fashion, claimed to see signs of that atavism in the shape and size of criminals' bodies. Likewise, the body of the white man spoke unambiguously to the scientists of the day of his cultural, evolutionarily guaranteed superiority over his atavistic cousin, the black man. Man's superiority over woman was written on their respective bodies in a similar way, while the earliest forms of child psychology found evolutionary principles at work when they saw children, with their large mouths, eyes wide apart, flat noses (resembling savages), turn into adults. The journey from child to adult, for this way of thinking, was the same as that from savagery to civilisation. The idea that ontogeny recapitulates phylogeny has never really gone away, and, through the work of Piaget, informs much contemporary developmental psychology.

What we can glean from this nineteenth-century anthropology and the disciplines such as criminology and psychology which were eventually linked to it, is that culture was always theorised in practical intellectual fields – never as an abstract problem. Culture was seen as a governmental problem, part of the field of social order. For example, anthropologists of the late nineteenth century, like Tylor, were fully involved in colonial policy, constantly lobbying for an Imperial Bureau of Ethnology which would collect knowledge and advise colonial administrators. While our earliest cultural scientists understood the heterogeneity of culture, they were also very clear about which forms of culture should be valorised.

Later on, Cultural Studies would become a field of inquiry which obeyed almost perfectly Foucault's famous notion of 'reverse discourse': culture, formed as a problematic intellectual and governmental object, was revisited in an almost Bacchic celebration of resistance, anarchy and class struggle. The Birmingham School, which we shall discuss shortly, turned around the nineteenth-century pathologisation of the savage, the poor, the black, the woman, reversing the morality of their intellectual predecessors as they sought to free 'low culture'. But let us not jump ahead too far. If we return to our description of culture as defined in the field of anthropology and sociology, we can see some other important moves that were to shape the direction of Cultural Studies.

The evolutionists did not have it all their own way at the end of the nineteenth century and in the early twentieth century. They faced the strongest challenge from the diffusionist anthropologists, of whom the most famous was Henry Pitt Rivers (see, for example, Pitt Rivers 1922, 1934, 1939; but see also Boas 1920, 1938; Smith 1928). The diffusionists argued that the evolutionists were wrong to see cultures all over the world going through the same process, albeit independently – any similarities between cultures, they insisted, were the result of diffusion between cultures. Diffusionists held that there had been one originary civilisation – Egypt was the strongest candidate for this role (see Smith 1931, 1933) – which had been carried elsewhere (diffused) and adapted to local conditions. Usually this adaptation had led to degeneration, but in Europe – happily for the European diffusionists! – the originary culture had been improved upon. This was an important break with evolutionism because it stressed degeneration as a normal part of cultural history; for the evolutionists, degeneration could only be seen as pathological.

While the diffusionists did not generate an especially different approach to governmental problems (from that developed by the evolutionists), two elements of their theorisation of culture are especially important to our story. First, it sowed the seeds for a functionalist approach to the study of culture. Pathology became a possible object of study (Durkheim performed the same service for sociology at about the same time). Second, it allowed for the theorisation of culture to embrace discontinuity as well as continuity. While Pitt Rivers and the other diffusionists were still evolutionary theorists, they introduced a Mendelian element into an otherwise Darwinian story (although once again we should stress that the evolutionists did not do justice to Darwin's theory, and generated a rather crude Darwinism to serve their purposes).

By the 1930s, functionalism had come to play an increasingly dominant role in anthropology. Scientists such as Bronislaw Malinowski (see 1926, 1984) started to understand individuals' modes of thinking as collective representations imposed upon them by their society. An individual's biology might have an impact on this (for example, all cultures have to learn to manage childbirth or death), but in general individual responses were simply a result of cultural conditioning. This extreme form of social determinism was shared in the cognate discipline of psychology – what Malinowski and others saw in strange cultures, Watson, Skinner and the rest saw in Western culture. It is worth pointing out in passing that anthropology and psychology developed in tandem over this period – a small piece of evidence to this effect is that Pitt Rivers played a central role in setting up the *British Journal of Psychology*. As we saw earlier, Margaret Mead made use of this perspective to argue that culture is learned.

Now the ground had been laid for a Cultural Studies which regarded culture as a series of structures, imperceptible by actors yet providing the limits and possibilities for individual action and social change. This can be seen in the specific treatment of culture in the field of anthropology, but it is also true that since this orientation was shared by many of the social sciences, it was a readily available resource for the new field of Cultural Studies. Anthropology, as suggested above, developed within an area demarcated by the twin problems of culture and social order. It was always, then, a practical enterprise, concerned with how knowledge might be derived from actual, governmental problems, and then turned back upon those problems to transform them. For example, both the evolutionist and the diffusionist anthropologists demonstrated how primitive cultures are always 'at risk': evolutionists showed how primitive peoples' lack of rationality put their societies at risk, while diffusionists showed how primitives are the same as Europeans and are thus prone to psychological breakdown in the face of catastrophe. Both claim a special role for anthropological knowledge in governing. The question of governing suffuses anthropology, such that the question of order and civilisation is ultimately more important than the study of 'otherness': indeed, anthropology was even considered to have something to say in the debate over Irish Free Rule.

The version of governing that these early anthropologists elaborated was liberal – and found liberalism in the strangest places. For example, E.B. Tylor studied the aboriginal Tasmanians, whom he regarded as the most primitive people ever encountered by contemporary observers. The death of the last full-blooded Tasmanian in 1876 was proof for Tylor that truly primitive people were doomed to extinction: the primitives' lack of reason was seen as their Achilles' heel. Yet he saw in the primitive people evidence for the rightness of the liberal state. Primitives were believed to possess the good qualities of natural democracy, courage in adversity, and strong family loyalties. The claim that humans were naturally social and co-operative allowed the idea that primitives could develop (with help from the anthropologists, of course) higher standards of rationality and morality with the appropriate institutionalisation of government, charity, justice, and so forth. The noble savage was already imbued naturally with a series of virtues, and the scientists of the age knew that the 'natural' progression from family to clan to tribe to nation, based on these human virtues of democracy, loyalty and so forth, could be gently guaranteed.

Cultural Studies: anthropology of home?

While the problem of culture was first addressed in anthropological circles, focusing on exotic societies, eventually an anthropological eye was turned on 'home' societies. It became possible to ask 'cultural' questions about 'civilised' society, and in Britain this research gathered itself around the 'Birmingham School', or the Centre for Contemporary Cultural Studies (CCCS), founded at Birmingham University in 1964. Richard Hoggart, Raymond Williams, E.P. Thompson and Stuart Hall were all associated with the CCCS at one time or another, and between them produced a distinct Cultural Studies which was later to be exported to other parts of the globe and modified for local conditions.

As 'founding fathers' of Cultural Studies, both Hoggart and Williams attempted to identify 'culture' within their own British society. For Hoggart and Williams, the overriding focus was on the split between 'high' and 'low' culture and on defending the worth of the latter. Hoggart, for example, identified an authentic working-class culture which was being endangered by a banal mass culture imported from the USA (Hoggart 1957). It is worth pointing out that to a certain extent, this emerging tradition relied on the mass culture studies of the Frankfurt School, even though this resource was often not explicitly acknowledged or was even derided (Kellner 1995).

Williams (1958, 1961) developed these themes in a similar direction, arguing simultaneously for a kind of cultural relativity – he focused on the different ways values are assigned to culture – and for a typically Marxist theory of the perfectibility of the human being (and hence of culture). Williams borrowed Marx's story about the evolution of society and the eventual disappearance of the class system, but rewrote it with culture as the central actor. Nonetheless, Williams's 'cultural materialism' was not about the inevitability of the evolution of culture – Williams moved away from Tylor and the anthropological approach – but about the various materially located possibilities for its development. Gramsci's (1978) work on hegemony featured heavily in Williams's analysis of the various arenas of culture, as he (Williams) spoke of three types of cultural forms – the dominant, the residual and the emergent – that struggled for supremacy, and whose interrelations generated new forms of culture. Dominant cultural forms were those which were an expression of the values of the ruling order, and so, through culture, the ruling order could make its values seem natural and timeless. Residual cultural forms were the historical resources available to cultures – no longer dominant, but still influential. The emergent cultural forms were the points of resistance and innovation, where new cultural forms could either challenge the status quo or be incorporated within it.

The CCCS focused in the main on this latter category of emergent cultural forms – mods, rockers, bikers, punks and others. The CCCS approach quickly came to regard (sub)cultural expression as a form of resistance – resistance through rituals, as Hall and Jefferson (1976) put it. By now, the distinction between high and low culture was taken as an area for study, not as a demarcation of the proper limits of Cultural Studies.

E.P. Thompson's important (1968) work on the English working class, tellingly entitled *The Making of the English Working Class*, played a crucial role in this legitimisation of what had previously been seen as 'low culture' and infra-academic. In particular, Thompson stressed the difference between a culture made *by* the working class and one made *for* it. His stress on agency as an historical force meant that he was the exemplary figure to be thrust into a debate about structuralism and determinism with the leading French Marxist of the time, Louis Althusser, who likewise stood in for an entire intellectual tradition. We return to this important debate shortly; for the time being, we stay within Britain.

Before we take this British theme further, allow us to summarise some of the key features of the type of Cultural Studies we are outlining for you (and some of our objections to it). As the driving force of this approach, 'culture' refers to the way of life of a group (including, possibly, a society), including the meanings, the transmission, communication and alteration of those meanings, and the circuits of power by which the meanings are valorised or derogated. By analogy, 'Cultural Studies' involves the study of a group's way of life, particularly its meanings (including its morals and its beliefs), with an emphasis on the politics of the ways those meanings are communicated. Cultural Studies must concern itself with the control of meanings and their dissemination, that is, with circuits of power and with forms of resistance.

For us, the study of meaning is a problematic element in this type of Cultural Studies. It is not altogether clear what boundaries can be erected around Cultural Studies – what counts as fair game, and what meanings belong to other fields. This lack of a 'pragmatics' for Cultural Studies, as Tony Bennett (1998) has put it, weakens Cultural Studies because it makes research questions virtually boundless, and leads the researcher into rather unfocused criticism of 'society' – a problem nicely underscored by McHoul and Miller (1998: ix–x):

> An everyday event . . . becomes *spectacular*. It becomes, that is, a form of 'popular memory', 'meaning construction' and so on. . . . The connection, then, is *speculative*: it is unable to show exactly how a certain kind of [Cultural Studies object] is actually so deeply and 'hotly' political; or how exactly it articulates with . . . broader sociopolitical agendas. And it is speculative because it simply assumes that the everyday event *represents* [a] . . . much broader field.

This type of Cultural Studies, this is to say, has difficulties of scale, moving effortlessly from the micro to the macro, seeing politics and power everywhere. It is not surprising that this type of Cultural Studies is so frequently anti-empirical (McHoul and Miller 1998: xi). Empirical work would get in the way of this grand theorising, this relentless induction and deduction. This lack of discipline on Cultural Studies' part we take to be a fundamental condition of possibility for its obsession with a search for meanings and for a desire to arrange all social meanings as a prelude to interpreting and judging them. The desire for deep meanings that are fit to be judged is, of course, the point at which Cultural Studies' obsession with meanings becomes its obsession with power. This style of engagement with power further weakens the discipline and sets it adrift in a world of baseless grand theorising.

British Cultural Studies and politics

Our brief survey has shown something of the intellectual roots and for-mative years of Cultural Studies, as it inherited mainly anthropological definitions of culture and then extended those definitions to an engage-ment with the culture or cultures of home. Early 'Cultural Studies proper' in Britain was never very far from leftist, usually Marxist, thought, and consequently the themes of dominant and resistant cul-tures, cultural imperialism, and the valorisation of 'low' culture were all foregrounded (hardly surprising, given what we said above about its obsession with power). Stuart Hall's work has long been directed at the necessary antagonism between academic work and politics. For Hall, it is impossible for Cultural Studies to be purely academic; it must also be the intellectual means for political activity.

Hall is perhaps the most strident critic of the institutionalisation of Cultural Studies, preferring instead a vision of extra-disciplinary studies of culture – politics by other means (Hall 1992). For Hall, Gramsci pro-vides a kind of hero-exemplar for intellectual work – the organic intellectual informing and informed by (class) political struggle. But Hall's work is much more than just a modified Gramscianism. A read-ing of Hall's prodigious output over the past 20 years reveals in microcosm some of the disparate elements from which Cultural Studies has been built. His work is basically Marxist, yet his careful engage-ments with and borrowings from scholars such as Barthes, Althusser, Foucault, the sociological subcultural and deviance tradition (Goffman, Becker), as well as linguistic and media theory, have furnished both him and Cultural Studies more generally with rich resources for analy-sis and political action.

However, at this point we must pick a bone with Hall's inter-disciplinarity in particular and Cultural Studies' inter-disciplinarity more generally. It has meant Cultural Studies has enjoyed (or endured) an enormous expansion in its field of objects. Virtually everything is cul-ture, so virtually everything can be studied, from women's magazines to shopping to manners to . . . well, you name it. Add to this the legacy of British Cultural Studies' insistence on the political content of all cultural objects, and the importance of Cultural Studies as a discipline of resis-tance, and you have a situation in which power, oppression, class and exploitation are everywhere. Suddenly, all the cultural practices which we have grown up with (or at least the human and the social bits of them) are labelled political and their collaboration with the forces of evil are rendered explicit. There are two obvious problems with this. First, is it *empirically* the case that everything is tainted in this way? Second, does not the ubiquity of politics in this view eventually come to trivialise politics? That is, if politics is everywhere, is it even worth remarking upon any more? We do not wish to excise politics from our new version of Cultural Studies (as can be seen in our analysis in Chapter 4), but we do not wish to see politics everywhere.

A trip to the continent: Gramsci, Foucault, de Certeau

British Cultural Studies, as we have seen, developed in the 1960s and 1970s into a discipline which sought to analyse two topics: meanings and their communication on the one hand, and power on the other, but hand-in-hand. To a certain extent, British Cultural Studies' engagement with continental European thought provided elements of this dual focus as well as strengthening the elements of it that already existed.

We mentioned the importance of Gramsci and his theory of hegemony above. Gramsci certainly furnished Cultural Studies with a way of linking the study of culture to the study of class society and thus enabled it to regard the search for deep meanings and the operation of politics as central. No less significant, however, was the model of intellectual labour which Gramsci provided. Gramsci's own biography – his struggles against Mussolini's fascism and his imprisonment – set him up as an example of intellectual labour as ethical labour, while his theorisation of the role of intellectuals as 'organically' part of their class or group, with a role in the political development of that group, inspired the British Cultural Studies movement to see their (primarily academic) labour as part of a class struggle. Gramsci's theory of hegemony also made it easy to see the culture of the dominant classes as universal and 'true'. Under the impress of this thinking and the thinking of the Frankfurt School, British Cultural Studies began to see mass culture as part of the political process – a way in which dominant ideas could come to hold sway. Cultural Studies, then, aspired to the role of the White Knight, able to dispute the meanings of mass culture and at the same time show how they could be replaced with 'authentic' meanings (the Glasgow Media Group's 'Bad News' series provides good examples of this kind of organic intellectual work).

Cultural Studies, then, in its British manifestation, has had a long-standing concern with politics and power. Given this concern, it is hardly surprising that Michel Foucault came to occupy a prominent position in the Cultural Studies' pantheon. The Foucault of *Discipline and Punish* (1977) and *The History of Sexuality*, Vol. 1 (1978) was read as a theorist of power. More specifically, he was read as a theorist who pointed to the omnipresence of power, and the need to analyse two neglected aspects of the field of power:(a) that power operates in local and micro-settings (in addition to macro-settings, such as the field of the operation of state power); and (b) that power is dependent on knowledge for its successful operation. This allowed Cultural Studies to use Foucault in proposing that power is even more ubiquitous than we had previously realised and that domination can and should be theorised as reliant upon efficient knowledge bases. From the second proposition flowed the idea that resistance to power can and should be theorised as a counter-knowledge. This twin boost to Cultural Studies propelled it into a series of studies of the local (what had previously been regarded as too mundane or trivial) in an attempt to reveal the 'hidden' workings of power, while simultaneously ballasting its claim to be an extra-disciplinary knowledge which could provide the intellectual conditions for political resistance. Gramsci and Foucault could thus be relatively easily elided. Indeed, Stuart Hall himself noticed this felicitous conjunction of the Italian and the French thinkers: 'Foucault and Gramsci between them account for much of the most productive work on concrete analysis now being undertaken in the field' (Hall 1980: 71).

Elsewhere, we have made clear our strong disagreement with this reading of Foucault's work (see especially Kendall and Wickham 1999: ch. 2 and ch. 5). In particular, we argue that Foucault's account of power simply does not work as a series of observations tacked onto an essentially late-Marxian conception of power and the state, a Gramscian conception of hegemony and an Althusserian conception of the relatively autonomous ideological state apparatuses which are nonetheless determined in the last instance by the economy. In many ways, however, our objection is beside the point: while the Foucault taken up by Cultural Studies is one we barely recognise, what is important is the effectivity that this (largely imaginary) Foucault had on the discipline.

In practice, what this meant was that Foucault was an inspiration to the Cultural Studies of the 1980s and 1990s, even though he was regularly criticised for lacking a theory of state power and for failing to pinpoint the causal connections between, on the one hand, the discourses and power relations he analysed and, on the other, 'big politics'. Stuart Hall, again, sums up this irritation, taking Foucault to task for failing to notice that all the shifts he outlines in his work 'converge around exactly that point where industrial capitalism and the bourgeoisie make their fateful, historical rendezvous' (Hall 1980: 71).

Foucault's work also gave momentum to Cultural Studies' turn to the everyday. Cultural Studies theorists now began to see power not just in the obvious places – in the Cabinet Office, in bureaucracies, in the education system, but also in the supermarket, the gymnasium and the car park. 'Disciplinary time and space' became inescapable as Cultural Studies threatened to turn into the discipline that would prove that George Orwell's *1984* was now a reality. However, Foucault on his own could not provide enough material to launch this kind of Cultural Studies of the everyday. Michel de Certeau was to provide a vital element in the soup that Cultural Studies fed upon.

In essence, de Certeau (1984) argues that people engage, through their everyday practices, with the world of consumption and in so doing fashion something individual and creative. De Certeau's emphasis is on the manufacturing of a series of resistant practices and with this in mind he distinguishes between 'strategies' and 'tactics', the former being the province of the powerful, the latter the response of the underdog. The powerful, who control spaces and architectures, invoke a series of strategies designed to order the less powerful; the less powerful make use of tactics, which tend to be much more about time than space, to resist the strategies and invent their own creative existence. De Certeau, for example, discusses 'idle walking', a playful, not necessarily logical, resistant, time-bound practice which opposes the strict strategic demands of orderliness of everyday architecture (see also Buck-Morss 1986).

De Certeau's approach receives perhaps its most trenchant criticism at Tony Bennett's hands (1998: 174ff.). To be brief, we agree with Bennett on the following points: that de Certeau lacks any kind of historical or sociological account of the social location of everyday practices; that de Certeau seems to equate all forms of 'transgression' or 'otherness', which essentially collapses all his 'tactics' into a single politics of otherness (see also Morris 1990); and that de Certeau regresses to a kind of Hobbesian view of power in which power is the prerogative of the rulers (the organisers of space) (see also Frow 1991), while nomadic and monadic subjects engage in a futile set of tactics, 'stripped of all weapons except guile, ruse and deception' (Bennett 1998: 177). (As noted earlier, we offer our account of the culture of the everyday in a later chapter.)

Moving elsewhere: Cultural Studies the traveller

So far we have seen that Cultural Studies emerged from a variety of intellectual sources but was given a disciplinary momentum (while paradoxically resisting that momentum) by the British Cultural Studies movement of the 1960s and 1970s. We have also seen that while Cultural Studies established itself in Britain, it was assembled from a variety of international resources. Cultural Studies did not, of course, remain a purely British academic endeavour, finding a home in a variety of other settings, all the time adapting itself to local conditions. It is instructive to look at some of these local variants.

We start with Cultural Studies in the USA. To a certain extent, when British Cultural Studies found its way across the Atlantic, especially from the late 1970s onwards, many of the overriding concerns of the Birmingham School were lost on the journey. The interest in class seemed less relevant in America, and US Cultural Studies was certainly not shy about proclaiming its status as an authentic academic discipline. The birth of US Cultural Studies coincided with the postmodern critiques of Marxism, which allowed the work of Lyotard, Baudrillard and Derrida to become central to this new brand of Cultural Studies. US Cultural Studies maintained the project of expanding the range of topics to be studied, but frequently left behind the British injunction to attach these objects of study to 'big' political problematics.

For example, a casual look at some recent US Cultural Studies texts designed for teaching (see, for example, Alexander and Seidman 1990; Berger 1998; Mukerji and Schudson 1991) reveals an interest in popular culture ('Wayne's World', 'The Terminator' and 'X-Files' are all dealt with in Berger's text) but with an emphasis on demonstrating the play of signification, the complexity of meaning, and so forth. But this is not the full story, which seems to involve a later 'discovery' of power and politics. Diana Crane, in her useful survey of the teaching of the sociology of culture in the USA (1995), suggests that while Marxism has declined as a theoretical orientation in Cultural Studies, to be replaced by postmodernism, the links between culture and power or culture and politics have become the new 'hot topics'.

Crane provides some interesting tables to back up this view. Here are two of them:

TABLE 1.1   Frequently used theoretical orientations, 1989 vs. 1995

1989	1995
Production of Culture (19)	Postmodernism (14)
Marxism (9)	Symbolic Boundaries (13)
Structuralism/Semiotics (8)	Production of Culture (11)
Symbolic Interactionism (6)	Critical Theory (11)
Critical Theory (5)	Structuralism/Semiotics (9)
Functionalism (5)	Symbolic Interactionism (8)
Symbolic Boundaries (5)	Cultural Studies (5)
	Marxism (5)
	Poststucturalism (5)

Note: Theoretical orientations appearing in 5 or more syllabi; numbers in brackets indicate numbers of lists citing each orientation.
Source: Crane 1995: 2

TABLE 1.2   Frequently used themes and topics, 1989 vs. 1995

1989	1995
Culture and society (13)	Culture and politics/power (13)
Meaning, symbols (13)	Gender, ethnicity, race (12)
High culture vs. popular culture (12)	High culture vs. popular culture (11)
Mass communication, media (11)	Meaning, symbols (11)
Culture and social change (7)	Mass communication, media (10)
Audience characteristics, choices (6)	Culture and class (8)
Gender, ethnicity, race (6)	Method, measurement (8)
	Collective memory (6)
	Culture and society (6)
	Reception studies (6)

Note: Themes and topics appearing in 6 or more syllabi; numbers in brackets indicate numbers of lists citing each orientation.
Source: Crane 1995: 4

From the data behind these tables, Crane argues that British Cultural Studies remains peripheral to the US sociology of culture. British sub-cultural theory, as represented by scholars such as Hebdige and Fiske, appeared on several of the text lists she analysed, but Stuart Hall's work, especially his approach to the study of the media, has had virtu-ally no impact in the USA (Crane 1995: 3).

Of course, the sociology of culture is not identical with Cultural Studies. We might expect sociologists to have a greater concern with power and politics than Cultural Studies scholars from, say, an English department. Nonetheless, using Crane's evidence it seems plausible to suppose that US Cultural Studies is a repetition of the British attempt to link culture with power and politics, albeit after a slight time-lag. But we must add a rider: in the USA, the attempt has been to forge new forms of political criticism from a postmodern theoretical approach. Instead of the British interest in class, US scholars are busy developing new forms of the political analysis of culture based espe-cially on race and gender. The evidence that postmodernism is the forebear of this orientation is also provided by Crane, who notes the striking increase in European theorists cited in her sample of syllabi – virtually no Europeans made it to the 1989 list, but by 1995 half of the frequently cited scholars were European theorists and philoso-phers (Crane 1995: 1).

US Cultural Studies, then, seemingly had (at least some of its) origins in the British variant, but eschewing British political concerns it quickly developed its own obsession with power and politics. A leading light of US Cultural Studies, Fredric Jameson, in his review of the field and his subsequent debate with the Australian-based cultural policy theorists Tony Bennett and Ian Hunter, provides some more evidence that US Cultural Studies is now grounded in the analysis of power (see Jameson 1993 cited in Bennett 1998; Bennett 1992, 1998: 31–5; Hunter 1992). In this debate, Jameson defends Stuart Hall's vision of Cultural Studies as a kind of Gramscian venture in which the discipline becomes linked to political interest groups. Jameson also foregrounds this political engagement and suggests that concern with disciplinary boundaries and definitions is a relatively unimportant task. Bennett and Hunter, in their different ways, argue against the usefulness of a Gramscian model of organic intellectual work (both opting for, although not mentioning explicitly, the Foucaultian model of the specific intellectual). They follow this up with a plea for Cultural Studies to become much more policy oriented – to concern itself with actual programmes of government as they impinge upon and are shaped by culture.

This debate is exemplary: it shows us the repugnance felt in US Cultural Studies about the 'selling out' of Cultural Studies; but it also shows one of the Australian variants of Cultural Studies, the one especially associated with the Griffith University cultural policy theorists. These scholars took up Foucault's work, especially his few sketchy but immensely suggestive writings on liberal governance, to study and advocate culture as cultural policies which engage with the practices, programmes and agendas of liberal governance – the ways in which liberal governance works, not by using the state as an instrument of domination, but by governing *through* society and *through* culture.

This Foucault-inspired cultural policy work of the Griffith School is by no means the only version of Cultural Studies that has emerged from the Antipodes (and, it must be added, not all of them are as sympathetic to the Griffith line as we are). An overriding concern of Australian Cultural Studies has been with the category of national identity, especially an identity forged in the context of a colonial history (see, for example, some of the chapters in Frow and Morris 1993), though it has to be said that this trend can be seen elsewhere, and has perhaps gathered momentum as studies of 'the other' have become more popular in the wake of postmodernism and the new kinds of questions it opened up. Canadian Cultural Studies has in many ways a similar trajectory to its Australian cousin, with much useful work on cultural policy and communications networks, and with studies of national identity which seek to come to terms both with a colonial past and a (at least geographically) close relationship with a modern-day superpower.

However, it is in Asian Cultural Studies that question of otherness, identity and power have perhaps been most salient. It is hard not to see Edward Said's (1978) *Orientalism* as an exemplary text in this regard. Said famously described how Western imperialism still survives today, and although Said's book is mostly concerned with Islam, it is often used to understand the broader relations between the Occident and the Orient. 'Orientalism' refers to a universal discourse about the Orient that had been put together by Western writers, intellectuals and academics, and which provides the resources for the West's continued dominance of the East. The Orient was paraphrased, reduced and packaged into a series of convenient and portable belief structures which could be applied to all Arabs, all Indians, and so forth. While one of the most frequently heard criticisms of Said refers to a tendency to over-generalise from a case study of the 'Middle East', nonetheless his work provided the spur for a whole series of (more geographically specific) homegrown Cultural Studies of the East. Drawing not only on Said but also on the ideas of Mahatma Gandhi, Ashis Nandy and the long-standing academic Cultural Studies units in Delhi (the CSDS, the Subaltern Studies Collective and the Teen Murti), a specifically Asian Cultural Studies emerged which concerned itself with colonial and postcolonial identity, but also featured an engagement with ecological theory, especially under the impress of Gandhi's thought.

There has been a long-standing tradition of theorising 'otherness' in Asian Cultural Studies, a tradition that also features Occidental Cultural Studies. For example, Gayatri Spivak's work has travelled well beyond her native India to inspire especially British and US Cultural Studies; Homi Bhabha has applied a concern with otherness which clearly has its roots in colonial theory to the experiences of British blacks and what we might term 'Occidental others'. Similarly, in the USA, writers such as bell hooks and Henry Gates have opened up questions of black American identity. And the 'other', once revealed, proved to be everywhere, as feminist Cultural Studies and queer Cultural Studies, to name just two, opened up more and more questions for our, by now, global discipline. And while we are excited by the globalisation of Cultural Studies and the expansion of objects of inquiry, we are concerned that some of the characteristics of the parent that have survived – especially the obsessions with power and meaning – are an obstacle to Cultural Studies providing useful and accurate descriptions of culture.

Conclusion

In this chapter we have outlined something of the history of Cultural Studies, starting with some of the early attempts to study culture in anthropology. Cultural Studies had a 'virtual' existence in anthropology and the other human sciences, including the Critical Theory approach of the Frankfurt School, until the 1960s, when the Birmingham School gave it its own foundation story. Cultural Studies was then able to emerge as a discipline – even as some of its main figures shunned disciplinarity, which was associated with calcification and institutional surrender. Cultural Studies went through a series of migrations, and of course the geographically spread variants bumped into each other and the discipline changed and grew and cross-fertilised. Its fateful engagement with colonial and postcolonial theory, as well as with postmodernism, forced it to become concerned with otherness or alterity, but as we hope we have made clear, the whole enterprise has been held together by a concern with meaning and its communication on the one hand, and, on the other, the analysis of power and political strategy.

It is time for our new variant of Cultural Studies to be unleashed.

Not so fast. Unless you have slept through the chapter that has just passed before you, you will be wondering what happened to culture. We are writing a book about Cultural Studies, aiming to build a new approach to this discipline, yet so far all we have done each time we've hit the word 'culture' is criticise. Surely, we have to put our culture cards on the table.

Fair enough: for us, culture is ordering (yes, we like to have a three-word catchphrase). Our thinking is that even the most elegant definitions of culture – our favourite is Gellner's (1998: 186) 'the set of ideas shared by a community' – needs to have its eyes pointed firmly towards ordering, lest it be hijacked by the type of Cultural Studies we are arguing against. Any time and any place you find ordering, by our account, you have found culture. 'Culture' is one of the names given to the different ways people go about ordering the world and the different ways the world goes about ordering people. We cannot say any more now, as we have yet to say much about ordering.

2 The Notion of Ordering as an Organising Principle for Cultural Studies

'I just throw everything in the drawer!'

'What! You're crazy. I make sure all the knives of the same size have their own compartment, all the spoons, all the forks, all the tea spoons. I have different compartments for other sizes of each of these implements and a separate one again for those freaky little spoons like salt spoons, sugar spoons and mustard spoons. You can imagine how many drawers I need.'

'And you say *I'm* crazy.'

Both these folk are engaging in ordering – equally – even if they do not know it. They do it with their cutlery and they even do it with their conversational gambits and procedures as they talk about their cutlery. Government departments engage in ordering as they prepare a funding model for dealing with the unemployed. And so do those unemployed, even if they have to sleep in boxes because they do not have enough money to pay for better shelter. And so do fridges as they speak their own language of shelves and nooks and crannies. And so do you as you try to shove the large drink bottle into a space for a smaller one. And so do movies, with their scenes and sequences. And so do movie watchers, with their ways of watching. And so do books and so do readers. And so do those who think they do not.

Ordering is everywhere. Ordering is part of human life, whatever we think of it. The job of this chapter is to tell you more about ordering and to develop our theme that it is important for Cultural Studies because it allows us much greater access to the details of general and particular cultures and cultural objects and practices. If you think 'One Big Mac and a Coke!' is the only ordering Cultural Studies should be concerned with, then we want this chapter to expand your mind.

Here is how we go about this task. First, we expand our vision of the type of Cultural Studies we are aiming toward. Second, we define ordering and build on this definition. Third, we spend some time separating the notion of ordering from its close (but not always friendly) relative, order. Fourth, we spend a good deal of the chapter expounding upon the limits of ordering, even pushing those limits as hard as we can. This leads into a fifth section in which we turn from limits to the whole world, discussing how ordering relates to 'the world'. Finally, we pit ordering against ordering in dealing with the thorny issue of how ordering projects relate to ordering projects. We conclude by attempting to cement ordering in place as an object of study, the centre of our new version of Cultural Studies.

Ordering Cultural Studies?

When we talk of ordering cutlery, of ordering talk about cutlery, as well as of ordering by government departments, unemployed people, fridges, drink bottles, movies, movie watchers, books and readers, we are signalling a very particular direction for our treatment of these and other such objects and practices. We are thereby adding to our machinery of investigation, among other things, a Sacksian component.

To investigate ordering as a crucial component of life is a task made much easier by deploying at least some of Harvey Sacks's thinking, or at least Sacks as given to us by one of the great methodological synthesisers – David Silverman (we owe him quite a debt). In an excellent book that seeks to encapsulate and popularise Sacks's methods, Silverman tells us Sacks has

> a quite straightforward direction for research. We must give up defining social phenomena at the outset . . . or through the accounts that subjects give of their behaviour. . . . Instead, we must simply focus on what people *do*. (Silverman 1998: 48)

After noting Sacks's concession that this type of work can appear mind-blowingly laborious (or words to that effect), Silverman fully supports Sacks's claim that such work is anything but trivial: 'social order is to be found in even the tiniest activity. The accomplishment of this "order at all points" thus constitutes the exciting new topic for . . . research' (p. 48).

Clearly, Sacks's approach is very handy for us. We want to convince you that there is 'ordering at all points'. This sense of promise is enhanced by 'Sacks's example of how children learn what things mean and what is appropriate behaviour' (p. 59). Silverman summarises Sacks's findings thus:

> They [children] do all this despite initially having very little contact with the outside world apart from immediate family and its social circle. . . . [M]ost children '[turn] out in many ways much like everybody else'. . . . In other words, at every point, however minimal or seemingly trivial, children encounter social order. . . . [T]he nice message for novice researchers is that, in a sense, they will find evidence of social order wherever they look. (1998: 59)

Ah yes, Sacks gives us great heart:

> As Sacks puts it: 'given the possibility that there is overwhelming order, it would be extremely hard *not* to find it, no matter how or where we looked'. . . . Whatever our data, social order should be apparent. As he argues: 'tap into whomsoever, wheresoever and we get much the same things'. (1998: 59)

Sacks's battle cry for us to go forth and study ordering (he sometimes call it order and sometimes, adding a delightful twist, 'orderliness' [p. 126]), is a good point for us to leave the complex question of what Cultural Studies as the study of ordering might look like. We have not said much, but we have said enough to give you an idea of where we are heading (the Sacks/Silverman team return later in the book when we discuss everyday ordering in detail).

Defining ordering

By 'ordering' we mean, fairly loosely, attempts at control or management. Ordering, then, at least in the first instance, is very similar to the notion of governance, as developed by one of us elsewhere (Hunt and Wickham 1994; Malpas and Wickham 1995; Malpas and Wickham 1997). In this way, ordering, like governance, involves

> any attempt to control or manage any known object. A 'known object' is an event, a relationship, an animate object, an inanimate object, in fact any phenomenon which human beings try to control or manage. . . . [T]hink of any 'thing', 'object', or 'phenomenon'. Now try to think of this thing without the existence of thought (not only your own, any thought at all) about the control or management of that thing. . . . We suggest it is very difficult to do so. (Hunt and Wickham 1994: 78)

That will do for a working definition, but we need to nuance it quite a lot. The first task in this regard is to try to remove the possibility of your thinking 'obsession' each time we say 'ordering'. If any of you should think, from what we have said so far, or for reasons known only to yourselves, that our concern with the notion of ordering is a concern with some sort of 'fascistic' or 'anally retentive' obsession, we want to expunge such a presumption here and now. Ordering is not about dominating or even tidying, it is about acting on the world; dominance and tidiness are only two of many possible objectives for such action. From our point of view, freedom from dominance and messiness are equally objectives which must, for the study of ordering, be treated in the same way as dominance and tidiness.

Now back to the main story. If, as Malpas and Wickham suggest (1995: 47), ordering 'can be generalised to encompass all practices concerned with the control and management of things', then 'there can be no access to the objects' of ordering except through ordering. In other words, objects are given to us, as 'the world', only in and through ordering. As such, ordering can be considered characteristic of all human life. We shall return to this idea at many points in this book.

In formulating our ideas about ordering, we have made substantial use of the work of John Law. In his book *Organizing Modernity* (Law 1994), Law expends considerable energy in emphasising the need for a verb when exploring matters of organisation, management or government. He says 'the basic problem' of his book centres on the question 'What on earth is social order?' His first response to his own question is to throw out the notion of order. 'Perhaps there is ordering', he tells us, 'but there is certainly no order' (Law 1994: 1). Beyond this, Law proposes that we also dispense with the idea of a single order – *the* social order (p. 2).

Law is all too aware that the targets of our ordering – in short, the world – are 'complex and messy', that is, they are not given to ready and simplistic ordering (p. 5). Law recognises that too often the basic work of ordering – 'the heterogeneous but systematic infrastructural work of ordering' (p. 7) – is overlooked, dismissed as 'noise, as distraction, as technical failure or as deviance' (p. 7). Obviously, we are joining him in his quest to make ordering a much more studied phenomenon.

Law is more concerned than we are with the relationship between ordering and society, or 'the social', but we have little trouble extending his points on this issue to cover the study of culture. When Law summarises the relationship between ordering and society, we can readily substitute the word 'culture' for Law's use of 'society' or 'the social' and fully capture the import of his point:

> [Culture] is a set of processes, of transformations. These are moving, acting, interacting. They are generating themselves. Perhaps we can impute patterns in these movements. But here's the trick, the crucial and most difficult move that we need to make. We need to say that *the patterns, the channels down which they flow, are not different in kind from whatever it is that is chan-nelled by them.* . . . [Culture] is *not* a lot of [cultural] products moving round in structural pipes and containers that were put in place beforehand. Instead the [cultural] world is this remarkable emergent phenomenon: in its processes it shapes its own flows. Movement and the organization of move-ment are not different. (Law 1994: 15)

At very least, this helps our quest of defining culture by default – adding different descriptions of what culture might be without settling on any one, or even any group. We return to the question of how and to what extent ordering within culture forms patterns later.

Order versus ordering

We saw above that for Law ordering is not the same thing as order. Obviously we have much sympathy with these opening salvoes of Law – in many ways our book is also built around the distinction between order and ordering. However, we are not so fussy about the use of the noun form. By concentrating on ordering as we do, we would not be unhappy to see the notion of order (including social order) resuscitated where Law would have us abandon it altogether. For us, order can sensibly be thought of as a description of a state in which ongoing order-ing has made a situation relatively stable – in which ordering has become routinised (and we discuss this issue in more depth in Chapter 7).

Law is very keen for us to reject the 'purity of order', to break with the idea that if only societies were '"properly ordered" then all would be well' (Law 1994: 4–5). He believes that the desire for pure order is a 'mon-ster' – 'that what is better, simpler and purer for a few rests precariously and uncertainly upon the work and, very often, the pain and misery of others' (pp. 6–7). We think he is being slightly melodramatic here. Certainly it is possible, and worthwhile, as Law hints (p. 7), to investigate the ways in which some ordering projects of the nineteenth and twentieth centuries have involved much human suffering (he mentions aspects of capitalism and hints at Nazism and some forms of punishment). We would not have you steer away from confronting such 'monstrosities', but we do not tar every single attempt to achieve 'pure order' with this brush. Just as much as the 'nasty' examples may have been born of the desire for such order, so too may have been Edison's discoveries, or Crick's and Watson's, or any number of other projects which have had positive as well as negative consequences. To develop an example, think of the French urban reformer Baron Georges Haussmann (for more details, see Kendall and Wickham 1996: 209–12). It is difficult to avoid the conclusion that Haussmann's rebuilding of Paris, at Louis Napoleon's invitation, in the 1850s was based on a desire for 'pure order' (perhaps it is no coincidence that Hitler cited Haussmann as an inspiration) – out went narrow wind-ing streets, with their 'hidden' spaces, in came the grand straight boulevards that so define Paris today, and along with them vast amounts of parkland (47 acres in 1850 had become 4,500 by 1870) and a new sewerage system, among other changes. There can be little doubt that both Haussmann and Napoleon III saw these changes as instruments towards a new social order, one consistent with the paranoia of that state, a state especially keen to limit opportunities for internal dissent. But does this lessen the beneficial impact of the delivery of clean running water to nearly all Paris households, the development of an effective sew-erage system and the creation of all the new parks? We think not. The diagnosis of order is never that simple.

Moreover, even the most straightforward impositions of 'order' are not necessarily politically regressive. Collins and Makowsky, for example, describe a lack of order in Europe in the Middle Ages in the following terms:

Nor was there much order. Europe had been in continual warfare since the decline of the Roman Empire, and the threat of violence permeated everyday life. It was a world without police, in which individuals looked out for themselves. Towns locked their walls to keep out robbers, and masters could inflict harsh punishments on their servants, and fathers on their children. Torture was the common treatment for public suspects, and execution and mutilation were the punishments for trivial crimes. People knew their places only because they were kept in them; order existed only as violent oppression. (Collins and Makowsky 1998: 19)

While this account is undoubtedly exaggerated, it serves well to make the point that 'order' can be sensibly desired.

Law worries about the 'dreams of purity' of his own discipline – sociology (Law 1994: 8). While we acknowledge Law's wisdom in saying that it 'would be foolish for us to imagine that we are anything other than creatures of our discipline, and creatures of our time', we think, again, that he is worrying about purity of order unnecessarily. Whether it be sociology, Cultural Studies, or some other intellectual endeavour (be it a 'pure' science like mathematics or a populist pursuit like astrology), the point we made above against Law's tendency to dismiss all searches for 'pure order' is applicable here. Yes indeed, these endeavours can have ill effects which can sensibly be traced to their occasional searches for this type of order (Bauman's investigation of the role of social sciences in the Nazi holocaust [1989] is but one excellent source for this phenomenon), but some of their benefits can equally be traced to these searches. For us, as we discuss in some detail in Chapter 3, the appropriate approach to the study of ordering projects which have purist ambitions, and indeed to the study of all ordering projects, does not involve such overt judging.

The limits of ordering, or, ordering versus governance

In acknowledging above that our working definition of ordering accepts it as a rough equivalent of governance, are we proposing that ordering covers the same broad ground as governance?

'government', as in the rule of a nation-state, region, or municipal area; 'self-government', as in control of one's own emotions and behaviour; and 'governor', as in devices fitted to machines to regulate their energy intake and hence control or manage their performance. (Hunt and Wickham 1994: 78–9)

Not quite. While ordering covers this same ground, it might more accurately be said to treat control of one's own behaviour and emotions as an equivalent type of ordering to that involved in the rule of a nation state, region or municipal area, where the term 'governance' suggests that the latter type is more important than the former. However, in effect, this is a minor matter; the similarities between the two notions outweigh the differences. One crucial aspect of ordering that mirrors a crucial aspect of governance is its inherently limited capacity.

Ordering, like governance, is never complete; it always falls short of total control – it has some 'failure' built into it. This argument is quite complex. We rely on Malpas and Wickham to help present it (Malpas and Wickham 1995, 1997; only direct quotations from these two sources are acknowledged after this). It is not difficult for us to borrow some of their points about the limits of governance and convert them into points about the limits of ordering.

We can start with their basic point: 'we see attempts at control, which are constitutive of social life, falling short of their targets. There is no such thing as complete or total control' (Malpas and Wickham 1995: 40). Let us work through some examples.

Consider the project of ordering the world of the university. Attempts are made at different levels (individual, departmental, school or faculty, whole university, regional, national) to control a variety of factors – student quality, staff teaching load, staff teaching performance, staff research load, staff research performance, provision of professional qualifications for students, wider community service, and other demands made by regional or national governments (like taking in more school leavers to reduce youth unemployment figures), among others. These attempts feature various techniques – accounting, use of quotas, management techniques of encouragement and punishment, legal regulation, industrial negotiations, industrial sanctions, and personal disciplines, among others.

Limits are present in each and every attempt, in each and every technique. Every attempt falls short of its target in some sense or other. In some cases the limits may be subtle: a department might well achieve the exact number of students it sets for itself in a given year, but it is straightaway concerned to maintain that figure and/or defend it against the claims of other departments. Further, because ordering is never pursued in isolation – ordering projects are always the subject of ordering projects, and so on down the line – the department is concerned about the quality of its student intake and is subject to wider ordering measures which, sensibly, assume at least some failure in this regard. In other cases the limits are much more overt: individual staff members are constantly asked to quantify research output in line with an expectation that performance can be improved; senior university administrators try to run their universities in line with national governmental priorities, but must operate with the knowledge that they can never keep up with governmental initiatives; they, like all actors, are always chasing some objectives they can never quite catch.

It should be clear already that the limits of ordering are pervasive. Sometimes, as we say, they are subtle – as when ordering falls short of its mark because it is assessed from a perspective different from that of those directly involved in the attempt. Sometimes the limits are 'in your face' – as when things just don't work – but always they are there. To help ram this point home, we adapt a 'mundane' example in a bid to deal with the limits of the crucial self-control aspect of ordering.

Think about the pain (or pleasure) of ordering your keys. This ordering project involves attempts to make sure that your keys are readily available, that they contain all the keys you need, and that they are not lost. The techniques of ordering used here include the use of a key-ring, possibly some other 'finding' technologies (like a beeper), some disciplines of the self aimed at always keeping the keys in particular places (pocket, handbag, shelf) and perhaps a procedure for obtaining new keys as required and removing keys when no longer required. The attempts of course have their limits, usually in ways more annoying than spectacular: the keys occasionally or regularly not being where you remember leaving them; a particular key not working in the lock or at least being 'tricky' or 'sticky'; the key to the shed not being on the ring when you were sure it was.

The limits of ordering that we are discussing can be said to resemble the limits of a machine:

> Machines do not work perfectly or completely. Not only do they operate with some degree of inefficiency, but without constant care and attention they will eventually cease to operate altogether. Indeed, given the inefficiencies and breakdowns that are part of the life of any machine (and

modern electronic systems are no exception) it is perhaps ironic that the machine metaphor is so often used as a metaphor for unwavering control and domination. Machine metaphors should be understood as metaphors for imperfect attempts to regulate and control, attempts which thrive on both the regularity they achieve and on the ever-present knowledge that more regularity can be achieved. We pointedly reject the use of machine metaphors to indicate some hidden, all-powerful force intent on dominating us as an unwelcome 'big brother'. (Malpas and Wickham 1995: 42)

Another fascinating example of the necessary limits of ordering is given by Stephen Jay Gould who writes on one of his great loves, baseball. Dwelling on DiMaggio's famous 1941 hitting streak, Gould says:

> Probability does pervade the universe – and in this sense the old chestnut about baseball imitating life really has validity. The statistics of streaks and slumps, properly understood, do teach an important lesson about epistemology, and life in general. The history of a species, or any natural phenomenon that requires unbroken continuity in a world of trouble, works like a batting streak. All are games of a gambler playing with a limited stake against a house with infinite resources. The gambler must eventually go bust. . . . DiMaggio activated their greatest and most unattainable dream of all humanity, the hope and chimera of all sages and shamans: He cheated death, at least for a while. (Gould 1991, cited in Malpas and Wickham 1997: 92)

Gould's example helps us establish two points. First, it illustrates the inevitability of the limits of ordering, for even a baseball freak like DiMaggio could 'cheat' these limits for only a while – his remarkable capacity to order a baseball in ways few could, ran up against the limits of this ordering activity after 56 times at bat. Secondly, the DiMaggio example shows us that ordering is best understood as ongoing projects, rather than as an isolated or fragmentary event. DiMaggio may have been successful in hitting the ball and reaching base at different times, even in hitting a home run, but each 'at-bat' was and is measured against other innings and other games, in relation to a particular season, a particular career, and to American major league baseball more generally.

Our notion of the limits of ordering here takes us back to our earlier discussion of John Law, and in particular his preference for the verbal form 'ordering' over the substantive 'order'. To a certain extent our emphasis on the incompleteness of ordering – ordering as a process – reflects Law's point that order is a rarity while ordering is everywhere. However, as we discuss in Chapter 7, Bruno Latour's work allows us to think about the phase-transitions between order and ordering, or between order and disorder. Order can be attained when a 'network' (as Latour sometimes calls the social situations he analyses) is relatively routinised and stable. However, as we explore in more detail later, the oscillation between order and ordering, or between order and disorder, is a fundamental characteristic of the network.

But we digress. Let us take a brief detour into historical sociology to provide a different type of evidence about the limits of ordering. In his classic text *The Protestant Ethic and the Spirit of Capitalism*, Max Weber provides a well known historical illustration of these limits. In discussing the connection between religious change and economic development, Weber asks, 'why were the districts of highest economic development at the same time particularly favourable to a revolution in the Church?' He answers: 'the Reformation meant not the elimination of the Church's control over everyday life, but rather the substitution of a new form of control for the previous one' (Weber 1989: 36). He notes that this shift in control was a shift from 'very lax' control, 'in favour of a regulation of the whole of conduct which, penetrating to all departments of private and public life, was infinitely burdensome and earnestly enforced' (p. 36).

A summary statement about the role of Protestant asceticism makes a similar point:

> Christian asceticism . . . had, on the whole, left the naturally spontaneous character of daily life in the world untouched. Now it strode into the market-place of life, slammed the door of the monastery behind it, and undertook to penetrate just that daily routine of life with its methodicalness, to fashion it into a life in the world, but neither of nor for this world. (Weber 1989: 154)

In other words, the combination of religious and economic change brought about the establishment of a new system of ordering, yet this new system was characterised not by new levels of success, but by a new expression of ordering's limits. We are not imposing this point on Weber – he seems well aware of it, recognising, for instance, that the Protestant ethic was always limited in what it could achieve by way of ordering a population. After listing four 'principal forms of ascetic Protestantism' – Calvinism, Pietism, Methodism, and various Baptist sects – Weber notes many complex overlaps and differences between them. For example, there were considerable differences between Dutch and English Baptist sects at the beginning of the seventeenth century:

'The dogmatic differences . . . such as those over . . . predestination, were combined in the most complex ways, and . . . regularly . . . prevented the maintenance of unity in the Church' (pp. 95–6). Weber also directs our attention to the limits of the Protestant attempts to order the urge to acquire wealth. After pointing out that honest, disciplined, careful acquisition of wealth for its own sake was frowned upon, but wealth for the glory of God was encouraged, and noting that one result was a boon for the spirit of capitalism – 'accumulation of capital through ascetic compulsion to save' – Weber discusses two particular limits to the success of this attempt at ordering. One is that this ethic of wealth acquisition could not completely dominate competing ethical principles; in England, for example, the 'Merrie Old England' principle of acquisition for the sake of pleasure meant the Puritan principle could only be one of two major influences on the formation of 'English national character', not the sole influence it sought to be. The second limit to which Weber refers is closely related. It is that the development of rational, calculating character in the face of the temptations of wealth, so crucial for the development of capitalism, could not be achieved in every individual. For many, the temptations of wealth were too great. In this, the Puritans battled temptation in just the way the monastics did in medieval times (pp. 172–4).

We can leave the provision of examples for the time being and emphasise some general points that those offered so far have illustrated. Seeing ordering projects against other ordering projects, not in isolation, is necessary for a full appreciation of the limits of ordering. Separate instances of ordering might well appear to achieve complete or total control, but only if viewed in isolation. When one takes into account that the ordering project involved is itself subject to other ordering projects and they to still others, and so on, the idea of total or complete ordering becomes a chimera. 'Pure order' may prove a useful utopia which can inspire ordering projects, but it is unattainable.

In other words, ordering projects are always ongoing practices of ordering. All ordering attempts are aimed at the control of particular objects, yet no object is ever the target of just one ordering project and all ordering projects are themselves objects. So, in any array of ordering projects, any one of the projects is also the intersection of others inasmuch as each one is always the object of others. Ordering can therefore be described as an expansive and unbounded field in which diverse projects continually intersect, overlap and interfere. In this way, ordering is always a dynamic activity, in which objects are never completely controlled by any one project.

Yes, we are going so far as to say here that ordering resists ordering, that ordering produces interference between different ordering projects. Ordering always takes place in a contested space and, at the same time, paradoxically, the fact of such contestation makes ordering necessary. Objects are not compliant, ordering projects are continually disturbed, ordering is perpetual in that ordering is a continual battle against its own limits, against the possibility of its dissolution. Ordering projects, their limits, and the contests between them can never escape each other's company.

There is yet another twist in this twisted tale. In never having complete control of its objects, ordering can only ever address its objects in certain specific and partial respects, as we keep saying. But what we have not said is that this partiality of ordering is also a partiality of vision – ordering obscures the fact that ordering is limited and partial and so often appears to be complete, in its very incompleteness.

Law too recognises that incompleteness is a constant companion of ordering (Law 1994: 2). In applying this awareness to intellectual ordering projects, he says, 'we don't want to pretend that our ordering is complete, or conceal the work, the pain and the blindness that went into it' (pp. 8–9). In the wake of this expression of commitment to the idea of incompleteness, Law praises a particular type of intellectual story – one concerned with 'description of social processes'. He favours these 'stories' partly because 'they are less prone to heroic reductionisms' and partly because, in recognising their own necessary incompleteness, they are 'relatively modest, relatively aware of the context of their own production, and the claims that they make tend to be relatively limited in scope' (p. 9). These are worthy methodological features (non-features?) and we ensure that we include them in our methodological discussion, to be laid before you in the next chapter.

Pushing the limits of ordering

We might well have made clear that ordering has limits and we might well have made clear that these limits are complex, but we have not yet made clear what it is these limits are pushing against. That is, we have yet to address the question of the extent to which 'an outer limit' or 'outer boundary' affects ordering. To address this question we call on the help of both Foucault, especially his book *The Order of Things* (1970), and the German philosopher Martin Heidegger (in calling on their help we make considerable use of Kendall and Michael 1998, and Malpas and Wickham 1997; only direct quotations from these two sources are acknowledged after this).

The Order of Things offers an account of how the 'prose of the world', as Foucault puts it, was ruptured and reorganised by the intrusion of 'an anonymous thought from the outside'. We can take this 'outside' as Foucault's metaphor for the 'outer limits of ordering' we referred to above. In the closing pages of *The Order of Things* Foucault asks a very Heideggerian question:

> What is man's being, and how can it be that that being, which could so easily be characterized by the fact that 'it has thoughts' and is possibly alone in having them, has an ineradicable and fundamental relation to the unthought? A form of reflection is established far removed from both Cartesianism and Kantian analysis, a form that involves, for the first time, man's being in that dimension where thought addresses the unthought and articulates itself upon it. (Foucault 1970: 325)

Foucault further suggests that the post-phenomenological project (Heidegger is clearly Foucault's influence here, though he does not acknowledge it) can and should be read as 'an ontology of the unthought that automatically short-circuits the primacy of the "I think"' (p. 326). This 'unthought' is a necessary corollary of modern man, something which emerges at exactly the same time as 'Man' himself:

> Man and the unthought are, at the archaeological level, contemporaries. Man has not been able to describe himself as a configuration in the episteme without thought at the same time discovering, both in itself and outside itself, at its borders yet also in its very warp and woof, an element of darkness, an apparently inert density in which it is embedded, an unthought which it contains entirely, yet in which it is also caught. (Foucault 1970: 326)

This Foucaultian/Heideggerian idea of a limit that is both outer and yet within – 'both in itself and outside itself, at its borders yet also in its very warp and woof' – is ideal for what we are trying to get at in regard to the limits of ordering: always there, a necessary feature, yet dark and unseen.

Heidegger's account of the nature of technology is also suggestive of some important ways in which our account of the 'outer' limits of ordering might be developed. Heidegger directs his critical remarks about technology largely at the technological desire for completion and, in so doing, at technology's refusal to recognise its own limits. The bizarre point for us here is that the refusal to recognise limitation – the inevitability of limits – is actually a characteristic feature of ordering, as we hinted above. Heidegger's technology (*technik*) is, put simply, a particular form of ordering in which this refusal is all the more pronounced. Incidentally, in Chapter 7 we return to the notion of technology, and provide a more nuanced definition; however, for the purposes of this discussion, we do not yet need to dwell upon 'technology'.

Consider the liberal state as a highly developed and extensive form of ordering at the governmental level. In this way, this model of state ordering might be regarded as the most extensive and developed form of the technological. Yet, like all forms of ordering, and like all manifestations of the technological, the operation of the liberal state is characterised by ongoing limits, rather than by limitless success, even while it strives for greater and more complete control over its objects. As liberal bureaucracy hits the limits of its operation, however, it acts as if it does not recognise them, does not see such darkness within, going about its business treating the effects of the unrecognised limits as mere aberrations, to be corrected by improving technique. Of course, this means it does not see the limits as indicative of its inability to achieve any complete grasp of its objects.

We summarise much of the above by saying that Foucault takes from Heidegger the notion of limit as a different zone of thought, a burst of energy from outside, a form of shattered thinking, the very opposite of reason and yet its precondition; a limit is an 'other' to ordering that can take forms as prosaic as bureaucratic inertia or as startling as a wild, destructive act. Now we turn to the scope of ordering, to the fact that in one important sense, the targets of ordering can be summed up as 'the world'.

Ordering and the world

We can usefully begin this discussion with a point of Foucault about government: 'With government it is a matter not of imposing laws on men, but of disposing things . . . the finality of government resides in the things it manages' (Foucault 1991: 95). We can take 'things' to mean any object subject to ordering and as such we can be sure that 'things' are never 'completely determined' by ordering, they 'always extend beyond the scope' of ordering. The example of the university used earlier can be employed again here (in this section too, we owe a debt to Malpas and Wickham 1995, 1997; and again, only direct quotations from these two sources are acknowledged after this).

A university, with its students, staff, buildings and resources, is a target (or set of targets) for ordering. Of course, neither the university as a whole nor any of its components are completely amenable to the control of the formal governing bodies. Incompleteness is easy to see, sometimes as resistance, sometimes in other ways: staff refuse to abide by particular constraints on their teaching or research practice; student numbers increase or decrease independently of the relevant controls; the failure to complete a new building on time leads to a disruption in teaching schedules. Even without overt 'resistance', ordering gives rise to unexpected and unintended consequences, interference does its work. For example, the introduction of an early retirement package to open up positions for younger staff may turn out to be too attractive and result in a sudden shortage of more experienced staff.

In other words, ordering is never able to address an object in its entirety, ordering is only ever 'concerned with objects' in 'certain respects', ordering never grasps 'objects in their completeness', ordering in fact only goes after objects 'to the extent that they can be objects for' ordering (Malpas and Wickham 1995: 46–7). Now we come to a vitally important point in our argument – if, as Malpas and Wickham argue (1995: 47), ordering 'can be generalised to encompass all practices concerned with the control and management of things' then 'there can be no access to the objects' of ordering except through ordering. In other words, objects are given to us, as 'the world', only in and through ordering. *As such, ordering can be considered characteristic of all human life.* We can leave this point for now and say more about this complex relationship between ordering practices and the objects ordered by them. The most important thing to say is that the distinction between them – ordering and things ordered – is not a clear-cut one. No object is ever beyond ordering and, as this includes ordering practices themselves, as we discussed above in discussing the limits of ordering, we cannot hope to ever find pure 'things' or pure 'ordering'. Our investigations of ordering will always discover ordering techniques and the things at which they are directed mixed together. The very fact that the investigator can pull them apart for the sake of discussion or description is, of course, an act of ordering. Let us consider two examples.

The ordering of behaviour that is the concern of police forces and courts, with their associated bureaucratic-governmental structures, addresses the behaviour within particular 'frames', one of which in this example is 'criminality'. At a more mundane level, returning to those keys again, you might order your keys through a set of practices aimed solely at making sure you have them. Those keys are thereby addressed within a frame we might call 'items that must always be carried that can easily, but must not, be lost'. These objects – the criminal behaviour and the keys – are not, it should almost go without saying by now, ordered by these practices alone. Behaviour that is deemed bad is addressed within many frames other than criminality and keys are addressed within many frames other than your desire not to lose them.

This leads to the important idea that ordering is not merely constraint – ordering is productive as well as constraining. In this way, objects are constituted as objects, they actually become objects, through being addressed by an ordering practice – objects are objects through being ordered. But remember, every ordering practice is itself subject to ordering, and there is no need to posit an originary level for ordering: no such level is required and there are not even any levels of ordering and ordering systems, though hierarchies and patterns may be formed temporarily, as we discuss shortly. Some ordering practices appear to be producers from some perspectives, while others appear to be products. The fact that the perspectives are generated by and subject to ordering only means that there is no way out of this circle – it is a virtuous circle, the only vicious tendency being the desire to break out of the circle to find some foothold beyond ordering, which, for us, is simply a vicious type of ordering itself.

Ordering meets ordering

We have made it very clear that ordering projects are anything but lone wolves, but we have not yet told you much about the ways they hunt in packs. Law hints that ordering projects come together as 'social and organizational ordering'. He says that this type of ordering is largely about 'patterns', patterns that flow from stories – '*stories are often more than stories*; they are clues to patterns that may be imputed to the recursive sociotechnical networks' (Law 1994: 19). In this way, ordering projects form 'patterns in contingency'. Such patterns are not always easy to see. It seems that what he thinks we should be looking for are clusters of ordering projects that 'tell stories that connect together local outcomes' (p. 19).

It is by this move that Law introduces his notion of 'modes of ordering'. He says modes generate 'effects' by interacting with other modes (p. 20): the ordering picture becomes yet more complex. Law defines modes of ordering as, in part, narratives about the world. 'They tell us what used to be, or what ought to happen. Here there are ordering concerns, procedures, methods or logics, dreams of ordering perhaps, but nothing more. Certainly they are not pools of total order' (p. 20). We can only but agree with Law here; it should be clear that for us, too, ordering projects can only ever group in ways that confirm their limits – the meeting halls of ordering are definitely not rallying points for a march to total or complete control.

But Law goes on to argue that modes are also more than narratives:

> [T]hey are also, in some measure, performed or embodied in a concrete, non-verbal manner in the network of relations. . . . [T]hese modes of ordering *tell* of the character of agency, the nature of organizational arrangements, how it is that interorganizational relations should properly be ordered. . . . Indeed, it is perhaps in the telling that they first become visible. . . . But they are also, to a greater or lesser extent, *acted out and embodied* in all these materials too. I'm saying, then, that they are imputable ordering arrangements, expressions, suggestions, possibilities or resources. (Law 1994: 20)

Furthermore, modes of ordering are 'strategies'. Law warns that this notion needs to be handled with care, because it is too often taken to mean only the explicit plans of those involved in a particular ordering project. Law does not doubt the existence or the importance of this explicitly directed type of strategy, but he is adamant that modes of ordering are 'much broader' than this. In a way, their breadth comes from the fact that they are much less explicit than the strategies discussed above. He says they are much more like Foucault's 'discourses' – 'forms of strategic arranging that are intentional but do not necessarily have a subject' (p. 21, emphasis removed; see also Kendall and Wickham 1999: ch. 2, for a discussion of Foucault's usage of the notion of discourse and Foucault's approach to the problem of intentionality).

Law is aware that this way of handling the notion of strategy opens a can of worms: 'how wide can a "strategy" be? Is it not stretching the notion of strategy beyond all reasonable limits to impute strategies in the absence of knowing subjects? And is the notion of strategy appropriate at all?' (Law 1994: 21). Of course anyone working in any area influenced by Foucault's thinking would be all too familiar with these doubts (for just a few examples see any of the essays gathered in Gane 1986). Nonetheless, we acknowledge Law's originality in the way he deals with them. He suggests the main problem is one of 'imputation', that is of the way we interact with data. He says that by

> *imputing* ordering modes to the bits and pieces that make up the social . . . I'm saying that I *think* I see certain patterns in the ordering work of managers, and its effects. I *think* that if I conceive these patterns in this way, then I can say that they are being partially performed by, embodied in, and helping to constitute, the networks of the social. . . . And I *think* that it isn't so wide of the mark to assume that these modes of ordering have strategic (though possibly non-subjective) effects. (Law 1994: 21)

Moving further into the difficulties of understanding the relationship between different ordering projects, Law emphasises that we can say very little 'in general' 'about the relationship between modes of ordering, or of the effects that they generate and perform' (p. 22). This is an important insight, involving a warning to avoid *a priori* 'accounts of how well or otherwise the modes of ordering might fit together'. It is important in being sensibly limiting – 'We can't be very sure about what will happen when modes of ordering butt up together, until we see how they perform themselves in practice' (p. 22).

We do well to remember, in making use of this insight, that Law is offering it not long after telling us of the importance of patterns, that is, of 'patterns in contingency'. We are not suggesting any inconsistency here on his part; quite the reverse. But in pointing to the proximity of an argument that we should look for contingent patterns in modes of ordering to an argument that we should not take any preconceived ideas about patterns into our investigations, we are highlighting the delicacy of the position here. We absolutely agree with Law that ordering analysis has to identify patterns without inventing them. Our extra caution suggests that we think perhaps Law is not forceful enough in stressing that the path of particular pattern identification is a very narrow one and the fall into the valley of *a priori* imposition of patterns on sites being investigated is long and deadly.

Before we move on to consider the way clusters of ordering projects sometimes involve hierarchies, a consolidating pair of examples might be helpful. Consider, if you will, first, the management of a firm. Projects for ordering the work of the firm – say, producing plastic cups – are conducted alongside and as part of projects for ordering the firm's accounts, which in turn are conducted alongside and as part of projects for ordering the firm's relations with other firms, which in turn are conducted alongside and as part of projects for ordering the firm's relations with government regulatory agencies, which in turn are conducted alongside and as part of projects for ordering the firm's human resources, and so on. The overlapping ordering projects here form stories about the firm, stories that have currency within the firm and a wider currency as well. The currency of the stories-of-the-firm-formed-through-ordering is, at least in part, generated by the way the stories are imputed to 'socio-technical' networks, that is the way they function as stories of the firm *qua* firm, over and above the people who work in it.

The different overlapping groupings of ordering projects form patterns. They are contingent patterns, not *a priori* patterns – a pattern may be formed by the intersection of the projects to order relations with other firms and projects to order relations with certain governmental agencies (for instance, a pattern may form around discussions with other firms in the industry about a collective campaign to soften the effects of a particular tax being imposed by some regional governments but not by others), but this does not mean that this pattern can be assumed when examining similar firms in other industries. These contingent patterns effectively connect local stories (for example, stories about the effects of the tax in question on the firm's accounting requirements) with other stories (stories from other firms about the way the tax is forcing up the price of their product) to form larger stories (stories about the dire economic consequences that will follow if the tax is not repealed).

We may call the groupings of ordering projects *modes of ordering* – stories about the firm and the world, the way the firm was, the way it is and the way it ought to be, but definitely not 'pools of total ordering', not ways of fixing the place of the firm in the world, even if some stories pretend this is possible. Such modes are more than these stories about the world. They are also performed, embedded – the firm is a complex amalgam of manufacturing, storytelling, accounting, tax-paying, etc., and this amalgam is alive in its buildings, its computers, its machines for manufacturing the product, its daily routines; the modes of ordering the firm thus express themselves in these non-verbal and material ways. In being both the stories about the firm-in-the-world and the very ways the firm exists, the modes of ordering the firm can also be said to be strategies, both explicit, intentional strategies to do with imposing a direction of the firm-in-the-world and implicit unintentional strategies which express themselves, much more subtly, in the way the firm's performance is directed by its way of being in the world that is clearly beyond the reach of any one person within it, or any set of such persons. Of course these modes-of-ordering-as-strategies are not directly imputed to this way of being, but are, rather, imputed to present and recent managers and to the effects of their management.

While we can and have sketched the modes of ordering involved in this example, and while we could continue an analysis along the lines of this sketch, we cannot use this sketch as the basis for a general analysis of modes of ordering. We shall almost certainly face the temptation to do so, to use the sketch as the basis for a set of *a priori* claims about ordering to be used in future analyses, but even if we give in to this temptation, the most we shall ever be able to do is to offer these particular modes of ordering *as if* they are general. We may convince the many people who are so used to this sleight of hand they have come to accept it as genuine general analysis, but it would still be particular analytical sheep in general analytical wolves' clothing. To attempt to order a particular analysis such that it appears general is a particular act of ordering and cannot be otherwise, no matter how many people take it to be otherwise.

Now for the second example, this time focusing on ordering the self – the self dealing with illness. Projects for ordering one's intake of drugs are conducted alongside and as part of projects for ordering one's sleeping patterns, which in turn are conducted alongside and as part of projects for ordering one's relations with others, which in turn are conducted alongside and as part of projects for ordering one's eating regime, which in turn are conducted alongside and as part of projects for ordering one's thoughts, and so on. The overlapping ordering projects here form stories about the self, stories that have currency for the self and a wider currency as well. The currency of the stories-of-the-self-formed-through-ordering is, at least in part, generated by the way the stories are imputed to wider networks, that is the way they function as stories of the self *qua* any self, as stories that could be about *anyone*, over and above the particular characteristic of one's self.

The different overlapping groupings of ordering projects form patterns. They are contingent patterns, not *a priori* patterns – a pattern may be formed by the intersection of the projects to order relations with others and projects to order one's eating regime, but this does not mean that this pattern can be assumed when examining these others' relations with still other friends and their regimes for dealing with allergies. These contingent patterns effectively connect local stories (for example, stories about the effects of 'night shade' vegetables) with other stories (stories from magazines or TV shows about allergies and various food groups) to form larger stories (stories about the increasing dominance of 'yuppie-foodie culture', for example).

Again, we call the groupings of ordering projects *modes of ordering* – stories about the self and the world, the way the self was, the way it is and the way it ought to be, but definitely not 'pools of total ordering', not ways of fixing the place of the self in the world, even if some stories pretend this is possible. Such modes are more than these stories about the world. They are also performed, embedded – the self is a complex amalgam of drug-taking, storytelling, eating, relating with friends, etc., and this amalgam is alive in its house or flat, its kitchen, its household appliances, its daily routines; the modes of ordering the self thus express themselves in these non-verbal ways. In being both the stories about the self-in-the-world and the very ways the self exists, the modes of ordering the self can also be said to be strategies, both explicit, intentional strategies to do with imposing a direction of the self-in-the-world and implicit unintentional strategies which express themselves, much more subtly, in the way the self is directed by its way of being in the world that is clearly beyond the reach of any particular person's self. These modes-of-ordering-as-strategies are not directly imputed to this way of being, or are only usually so imputed via certain forms of therapy – rather, they are usually imputed to present and recent self-accounts.

And here too we must say that while we can and have sketched the modes of ordering involved in this example, and while we could continue an analysis along the lines of this sketch, we cannot use this sketch as the basis for a general analysis of modes of ordering.

Now back to our point about hierarchies. Law defends Foucault against charges that his notion of discourse 'cannot make sense of hierarchy and inequality'. Law thinks this charge wrongheaded, but says his main aim in mounting an argument against it 'is to show that a series of different ordering modes – which might indeed in some circumstances actually be in conflict with one another – may interact to perform a series of materials and material arrangements that have hierarchical and distributional effects' (Law 1994: 25). In other words, ordering can and often does involve hierarchies and, as such, ordering analysis should avoid the temptation to understand ordering activities as discrete activities that somehow all exist on the ground floor of a building, never able to relate to one another in a hierarchical way. To develop briefly one of the above examples, it would be absurd to suggest that all the ordering projects mentioned in regard to the firm-in-manufacturing operate continually on a flat plane. Sometimes projects to order the firm's tax relations dominate projects to order sales, sometimes the other way around, and sometimes they are both subsumed in a hierarchy of projects whereby projects to order the quality of the work environment rule the roost. There is of course no *a priori* way of knowing what a hierarchy of ordering will be, but no decent analysis of ordering can afford to ignore the possibility of hierarchies, or with it the possibility that every ordering dog will have its day.

Conclusion: towards an ontology of ordering

As should be clear from the above discussion, we privilege the notion of 'ordering', in particular in relation to the way in which a subject–object relationship can be conceptualised. It is no doubt worthwhile expanding on this issue, which we take to be connected to an ontology of ordering. First of all, our notion of ordering is, essentially, relational. That is to say, ordering can be conceived of as an *emergent property* of the relation between objects – conversely, objects only exist inasmuch as they are objects of ordering. Before we discuss the ontological nature of ordering, we should say a little about 'objects'. Much in the manner of thinkers such as John Dewey or George Herbert Mead, we take objects to be formed through a (social) relationship. As we have described above, objects only present themselves to us through ordering practices. Now this is not to take a social constructionist position on the existence of objects; rather it is to suggest that the character and qualities of an object are constructed out of the relationship between the object itself (what we might call its 'objectity') and the observer's action upon that object. We insist upon the symmetry of the relational dynamic between the observer and the observed, and, unlike the social constructionists, would not wish to give primacy to the observer in such a relationship.

Objects and observers, then, are locked in a relationship in which each has an effect on the other. This is, of course, not far from the principles of quantum theory, which theorise objects as probabilities whose character is determined by their interaction with an observer (crucially, how those objects are measured). While this notion of 'objectity' suits our purposes, we are intrigued by other work in quantum mechanics which stresses order or self-organisation as emergent properties of quantum systems (see especially Prigogine and Stengers 1984, 1997). For Prigogine and Stengers, order is conceptualised as an emergent property of a complex, chaotic system – a system which is chaotic insofar as it is in a non-equilibrium state. Two short examples should clarify this notion. Boiling water is a way of going from an equilibrium to a non-equilibrium state; as water starts to boil, it reaches the 'edge of chaos', and at this point it starts to self-organise – the convection patterns become regular, complex and ordered. In short, matter in non-equilibrium states gets 'channelled' toward states of greater complexity. The second example is what happens when a video camera is focused on its own monitor or output. This act, like the act of boiling water, allows us to view the transition from an equilibrium to a non-equilibrium state. Initially, the video monitor shows us something that looks like chaos, but slowly we see the display in the monitor settle down and produce regular pulsing and patterned routines. It is important to realise that these routines are non-determined, that is to say, they will vary greatly depending on the focus, the distance from the video to the monitor, light sources, etc. What we see in these examples, then, is the emergence of ordering from chaos, but an ordering that is essentially unpredictable (or contingent).

Now our purpose here is not to be positivist: we do not wish directly to apply the approaches of the 'hard' sciences to the 'soft' (even though it should be remarked that in principle quantum mechanics, and the rules of emergent complexity and self-organisation, are applicable to everything). However, we can follow through some analogies to gauge their usefulness for a possible Cultural Studies' ontology of ordering. Ordering can be thought of as something which emerges out of the relation between object and observer; however, this ordering is not easily predictable or determined, but rather is entirely *contingent*. As we trace the emergence of order through a temporal dimension, it is always the case that a variety of possible other outcomes could (but did not) occur. The history of ordering – ordering followed through its temporal dimension – is contingent inasmuch as it is something built on a series of *non-necessary* events. Gould (1989) has perhaps explained this most elegantly in his discussion of how evolution works – if we were to replay life's tape recorder once again, we should certainly not see the same results we now see. Life *is* ordered, but the ordering involved is contingent rather than necessary.

As you will see in detail in the next chapter, there is a methodological requirement that emerges from this perspective: description might be the limit of our analytical ambition. The systems we deal with (including cultural systems) are predisposed to ordering, but that ordering is entirely contingent, and thus can only be described *post hoc*. Prediction becomes impossible – or tightly limited, in any event. Once again, an example from the natural sciences might help to clarify this position. The weather is a well known example of a chaotic system: it is a system which is in principle predictable, but the possibility of prediction quickly disappears because there are so many variables that it is impossible for us to specify completely and correctly any momentary 'weather-state'. The fact that we are missing data on a variety of variables does not matter too much for a short time, but because the weather is an iterative system, the tiny and insignificant factors we neglect to consider (most famously, a butterfly flapping its wings in a distant rainforest) have an increasing effect on the developing system, such that it quickly becomes unpredictable. As Joseph Ford has glossed this, it means that computer modelling of the weather turns into nothing more than an attempt to xerox the current state of the weather system. While this sounds the death-knell for attempts to predict complex systems, it allows us to see that description of those systems becomes the proper end of inquiry. It might also be said that *post hoc* description which stresses the temporal development of a system can be seen as the richest form of description (for a similar argument, see Gould 1989: 277 ff.; for an investigation into these themes of iterative systems see Flaschka and Chirikov 1988).

We conclude from all this that not only is ordering a legitimate object of inquiry for Cultural Studies, it is an object that can sensibly guide the operation of the discipline – Cultural Studies as the study of ordering. Using a launching pad given to us by Sacks/Silverman and by John Law, we have sketched what the ground of this understanding of the discipline might look like, keeping a focus on the idea that ordering can be considered characteristic of all human life: hence our catchphrase that culture is ordering. We have defined ordering in terms of attempts to control all known objects. We have outlined the relationship between ordering and order. We have discussed the crucial fact that all ordering projects are necessarily limited, that total control through ordering is not possible, pushing this idea of limits as hard as we dare by calling in the aid of Heidegger and Foucault. We have also proposed that even in the face of these limits, ordering can reasonably be said to involve the ordering of 'the world'. We have set out the way ordering projects relate to one another, forming patterns and sometimes hierarchies. We have even proposed a possible ontology of ordering.

At this stage, as we noted, Cultural Studies as the study of ordering lacks a distinct methodology. We rectify that shortcoming in the next chapter.

3 Building a Method for Cultural Studies as the Study of Ordering

We start with a yet another warning: while this chapter presents you with a methodology for Cultural Studies as the study of ordering we do not think it is possible to give you a 'principled' methodology that can be uniformly and confidently applied to all situations and investigative possibilities – the idea of a recipe fixed in stone is anathema to the sort of Cultural Studies we have in mind. This is to say that our new direction for Cultural Studies privileges the careful and detailed 'unprincipled' study of ordering. Our emphasis, then, is on developing a means of careful and detailed investigations of ordering at work – a way of seeing cultural objects and practices in close-up, perhaps not quite as you have never seen them before, but in that neighbourhood.

Here is how we do it. First we discuss some ancient sceptics. We use this as a way in to our major methodological resource, one not so far discussed in the book – some beautifully formed moves designed by Ludwig Wittgenstein. This done, for the remainder of the chapter we use the ideas of a figure you have already met – John Law (with a little Bruno Latour and Michel Callon thrown in) – to ensure our method is capable of leading primarily to careful and detailed investigations. Through all this we offer three (yes, just three) firm suggestions to you, what we call methodological protocols. We offer them and try to tease them into a form that is both easy to use and consistent with the complexities of the moves one needs to make to undertake Cultural Studies as the study of ordering. We let them emerge from our reading of Pyrrhonism and Wittgenstein and slowly add to their bulk as we work through the Wittgenstein and the Law material, even though this allows them to become terribly overweight. In the conclusion to the chapter we put them on a severe diet, trimming them all back to a very minimal form.

Pyrrho as a basis for Wittgenstein

The work of Pyrrho of Elis is separated by 2,300 years from the work of Ludwig Wittgenstein, but we think it is not too difficult to build a bridge between them (and we are hardly the only ones to think so; see especially Toulmin 1994: ix–x). Taken together they provide an ideal means of producing a method that has us getting on with it – getting on with investigations of cultural objects and practices without being bogged down in concerns about methodological principles.

We shall not spend too long detailing the Pyrrhonian mind-set, fascinating though it is. We do not need much; we need only a brief summary of Pyrrhonian scepticism here to set the stage for our more detailed discussion of Wittgenstein's contribution. (Hankinson 1995 is a very good place to begin to look for more on Pyrrhonism; we are obliged to this excellent source, and we freely acknowledge that we do not do it justice, or the Pyrrhonism it presents so well.)

Pyrrhonism is not the only form of scepticism we modern Westerners have inherited from the ancient Greeks. Hankinson (1995: chs 1–8) works through at least five schools of Ancient Greek sceptical thought, most based in different eras, but with enough overlap to have produced not inconsiderable disputation between them, at the times of their development and after. Hankinson focuses most of his attention on Pyrrhonism, although not before pointing out that Pyrrhonism's long journey to the present has not been a smooth one; it is a journey on which its superiority over its rivals has not always been clear (pp. 9–12).

Pyrrho of Elis is thought to have lived and worked for much of the period between 360 and 270 BC. He wrote nothing, in line with his thoroughgoing scepticism, and the movement/school that bears his name has been constructed from fragments produced by his disciples and from a remarkable book from one of his later followers, Sextus Empiricus (p. 4).

Pyrrhonian scepticism is about more than the basic sceptical claim that we cannot know anything. Crucially, it adds to this claim (perhaps it is better to say it subtracts from it) that we cannot even know that we cannot know anything, an addition that entails a particular type of suspension of judgement. The scope of Pyrrhonian scepticism is, thus, very ambitious. One of the aforementioned 'fragments' reads:

> Pyrrho's pupil, Timon, says that anyone who is going to lead a happy life must take account of the following three things: first, what objects are like by nature; secondly, what our attitude toward them should be; finally, what will result from those who take this attitude. Now he says that Pyrrho shows that objects are equally indifferent and unfathomable and indeterminable because neither our senses nor our judgements are true or false; so for that reason we should not trust in them but should be without judgement and without inclination and unmoved, saying about each thing that it no more is than is not or both is and is not or neither is or is not. And Timon says that for those who take this attitude the result will first be non-assertion, then tranquillity. (cited in Annas and Barnes 1994: x)

Pyrrhonism, as this passage makes clear, is as much a way of life as it is a set of methodological moves. However, it is reasonable for our purpose simply to note this (albeit vastly) wider objective (we return to the idea of philosophy as a way of life later in the book, when we discuss the culture of the everyday) and concentrate on summarising just some of what Pyrrhonism has to offer our particular methodological requirements. We suggest we are being consistent with Pyrrhonian thinking in using Pyrrhonism for a limited purpose; we are offering no judgements in doing so, simply following accepted conventions of writing a book of this type.

Let us return to the remarkable Sextus Empiricus, a physician who is thought to have flourished some 500 years after Pyrrho (in the second century AD). He set out to capture in one set of writings everything there was to know about Pyrrhonism. While there has been considerable debate about the extent to which Sextus was an original thinker, there is no doubt that the survival of this set of writings, known to us as *Outlines of Scepticism* (we use the 1994 edition edited by Annas and Barnes), particularly its career since its 'readable Latin translation of 1562', has made it the key text of Pyrrhonian thinking (Hankinson 1995: 6–12).

Sextus relates a Pyrrhonism that demands we throw away all thoughts of revealing reality, yet also indefinitely continue our investigations. We are to proceed down this seemingly paradoxical path on the basis of the proposition that we can never deny the possibility of revealing reality. As we investigate, we must describe appearances:

> By way of a preface let us say that on none of the matters to be discussed do we affirm that things are just as we say they are: rather, we report descriptively on each item according to how it appears to us at the time. (Sextus Empiricus 1994: 3)

Herein lies Protocol One of our methodological approach – describe how things appear (and under 'things' we of course include cultural objects and practices). Pyrrhonism, in making this demand, is also demanding that we suspend judgement, or at least strive to do so. Easier said than done, of course. Sextus urges us, as a first step, to 'set out oppositions' – divide appearances (and thoughts about them) into one and its opposite. Keep doing this so that you get further and further from making judgements. This too, we hardly need tell you, is very difficult. We urge you to try it as an exercise (and keep on trying it), but it is the description of appearances that is most important to us here.

Appearances, for the Pyrrhonian sceptic, we stress, are much more a matter of 'seems' than a matter of 'is'; we are prepared to go as far as to say that 'seems' is as good as it gets – you should henceforth forget about 'is'. Take honey and its supposed sweetness: of course, honey appears sweet but, as Pyrrhonians, we are afraid we can not say whether it really is or is not sweet; we must toss this question, along with all others of this nature, on to the pile marked 'for perpetual investigation' (which means that we will forever suspend judgement about it). Sextus says that Pyrrhonian sceptics accept that appearances can guide us because they accept that we are capable of perception and thought (Sextus Empiricus 1994: 8–9). This means that they accept that we get hungry, cold, hot, and thirsty, but, more than that, they acknowledge that we have developed customs and laws and ways of dealing with life and they accept these too, as part of the package of appearances (pp. 8–9).

The limits of certainty meet the limits of doubt

In turning to Wittgenstein, we are not turning to his entire philosophical *oeuvre*. Rather, we are concentrating on a small but brilliant set of notes he wrote not long before his death, published later as *On Certainty* (1979). It is to this text that we now turn, armed with the first of our three methodological protocols, urging us to accept appearances, even those complex appearances of customs, laws and knowledge endeavours, and to concentrate on describing them as best we can.

Wittgenstein is firmly within the Pyrrhonian tradition in his handling of the notions of certainty and doubt and, moreover, his handling of the practices of certainty and doubt. In answering G.E. Moore's famous attempts to provide certainty (and a response to Moore is at the heart of *On Certainty*), Wittgenstein never allows certainty to lose sight of doubt and vice versa.

Let us begin by explicating Wittgenstein's account of what is actually involved in certainty. He builds his account through a series of hints. For example, he tells us that the difference between the concepts 'knowing' and 'being certain' 'isn't of any great importance'. In a law court, for instance, the two are interchangeable (Wittgenstein 1979: §8, 3 [NB: in the reference the section number is followed by the page number; all references to Wittgenstein are to this 1979 source]). Another hint involves behaviour or attitude (something very important for us, as will become progressively clearer): 'Certainty is *as it were* a tone of voice in which one declares how things are' (§30, 6). He also says that certainty can be about acting – 'I act with *complete* certainty. But this certainty is my own' (§174, 25).

We are of course getting closer to Wittgenstein's widely known use of the notion of language-games. Our purposes here do not include a full explication of this notion; we merely allow it to emerge in his 'hints' about certainty. Here is an example from relatively early in his book, in which he uses the notion of language-games to bring certainty and doubt together. To doubt the existence of the planet Earth, he suggests, is to engage in a language-game; certainty and doubt about such a matter are part of the game: 'This language-game just *is* like that' (§56, 9). We are being urged to accept the appearance of the object of our inquiry – in this case the planet Earth, but any cultural object or practice could be satisfactorily substituted here – without minimising the spur to investigation provided by the clash between certainty and doubt.

We are thus given Wittgenstein's endorsement of Protocol One of our methodological approach – describe how things appear. But it is worth stressing that for Wittgenstein, as for the Pyrrhonists, this is not a step towards explanation; we must add some weight to Protocol One here. Wittgenstein does not want us explaining things, but to get away from explanations in favour of descriptions – 'At some point one has to pass from explanation to mere description' [§189, 26]). So Protocol One now reads: describe how things (including cultural objects and practices) appear and in doing so be careful not to rush to an explanation of the things.

It should already be clear that there is, in this Wittgensteinian approach, a symbiotic relationship between certainty and doubt. Wittgenstein tells us that doubting is a game that presupposes certainty and that, consequently, to doubt everything makes it impossible to doubt anything (§115, 18). Our search for further methodological protocols in Wittgenstein's propositions is given a boost by his idea that doubts form a system (§126, 19). Systems of doubt are, we suggest, conglomerations of certain types of thinking practices. Seeing doubt, and other types of thinking, in systems helps in the task of close description of cultural objects and practices, to which we are dedicated in this chapter and in this book. So, this is Protocol Two of our methodological approach: thinking, including doubt and certainty, forms definite, and hence describable, systems.

Showing his Pyrrhonian direction, Wittgenstein allows us at least to begin to describe what might otherwise be too abstract, allowing us to glimpse a system of doubt/judging in some mundane practices of learning. "How do we know that someone is "in doubt"?' he asks on our behalf. Answer: 'From a child up I learnt to judge like this. *This* is judging.' 'This is how I learnt to judge; *this* I got to know *as* judgement.' He elaborates by making clear that experience 'is not the ground for our game of judging. Nor is it its outstanding success.' 'Men have judged that a king can make rain; *we* say this contradicts all experience. Today they judge that aeroplanes and the radio etc. are means for the closer contact of peoples and the spread of culture' (§§127–32, 19).

He gives us a further insight into this particular system when he argues that children learn facts well before they learn the reliability or otherwise of the tellers of those facts and in doing so they take in the assumptions behind the facts without learning them (for example, that a mountain has existed for a long time, taken in as part of the fact that so and so has climbed it). Children thus learn lots of things and fit them into systems, learning that some things in the system are more stable than others. Some things, then, are held as stable not by anything intrinsic to them but by what is held fast around them (§§143–4, 21). As Wittgenstein puts it in another context: 'We just *can't* investigate everything, and for that reason we are forced to rest content with assumption. . . . My *life* consists in my being content to accept many things' (§§343–4, 44).

We return to assumptions and judgements later. For now, we stick to what Wittgenstein has to say about the dance of doubt and certainty. He suggests that systems of doubt contain methods: he says that assertion (that is, asserting things as 'absolutely solid') is 'part of our *method* of doubt and inquiry' (§151, 22), and he helps us place doubt in systems of learning, to extend an earlier point, in telling us that children learn certain facts that they take on trust. As children learn by believing adults, we can conclude that 'Doubt comes *after* belief'; that is, things are accepted on authority and then confirmed or disconfirmed by experience (§§159–61, 23).

None of this is to suggest that our systems are particularly stable. For example, Wittgenstein argues that to doubt the existence of Napoleon is ridiculous, but to doubt that the world existed 200 years ago is worth considering, for this 'is doubting our whole system of evidence. It does not strike me that this system is more certain than a certainty within it' (§185, 26). In other words, certainty and doubt crucially, for us, involve a great deal of doing: 'it is not a kind of *seeing* on our part; it is our *acting*, which lies at the bottom of the language-game [of certainty and doubt]' (§204, 28); 'I want to say: it's not that on some points men know the truth with perfect certainty. No: perfect certainty is only a matter of their attitude' (§404, 52).

Doubt, then, has to be entertained in a particular way, to be held in balance with some certainty. This is to say, among other things, that to be 'reasonable' requires a mix of doubt and certainty: 'The reasonable man does *not have* certain doubts' (§§219–20, 29) (or as he puts it on other occasions, extending a point made earlier: 'A doubt without end is not even a doubt' [§625, 83]; 'A doubt that doubted everything would not be a doubt' [§450, 58–9]). Of course this does not mean that there is some eternal, universal standard of reasonableness. Wittgenstein is very firm on the point that there are no rules to determine which doubts are reasonable and which unreasonable: 'There are cases where doubt is unreasonable, but others where it seems logically impossible. And there seems to be no clear boundary between them' (§§452–4, 59).

However, at the intersection between reasonableness and doubt lurks the possibility of not being understood. Wittgenstein says, for example, that it is difficult to comprehend someone who doubts the existence of the world 100 years ago. He adds: 'I would not know what such a person would still allow to be counted as evidence and what not' (§231, 30). Another example he offers concerns the use of colour words: if someone doubts that an English pillar-box is red, he or she would be considered to be colour-blind, or to have an improper grasp of English, but if neither, he or she would not be understood (§§525–6, 69–70).

Wittgenstein extends this discussion by saying, 'If I wanted to doubt the existence of the earth long before my birth, I should have to doubt all sorts of things that stand fast for me' (§234, 31). He gives us a more than useful hint about the best way to handle this dilemma, a hint that we can add to our list of his hints about the role of behaving and acting – this time involving the notion of context:

> If I say 'an hour ago this table didn't exist', I probably mean that it was made later on. . . . If I say 'this mountain didn't exist half an hour ago', that is such a strange statement that it is not clear what I mean. . . . But suppose someone said 'This mountain didn't exist a minute ago, but an exactly similar one did instead'. Only the accustomed context allows what is meant to come through clearly. (§237, 31)

Similarly, he notes that although doubt has characteristic manifestations, 'they are only characteristic of it in particular circumstances' (§255, 33). For example, in regard to the colour of the English pillar-box again, after asking, 'Is it essential for our language-games . . . that no doubt appears at certain points, or is it enough if there is the feeling of being sure . . . ?' Wittgenstein says that whether someone has a doubt that something is red is not important. 'What is important is whether they go with a difference in the *practice* of the language.' Interestingly, he adds that even if the person in question has read some sceptical philosophy and approaches all discussions with a degree of practised uncertainty, the practice of language will have no difficulty overcoming this (§524, 69). We discuss context in more detail later, but we should not let it go here without saying that it forms a part of Protocol Three of our methodological approach – in describing how things appear, we should be aware that appearances appear in contexts (that the contexts involve actions, attitudes and behaviours, as the brief discussion of the colour red above indicates, is the source of an important addition to this protocol, but that can wait).

Wittgenstein elaborates his account of certainty in suggesting that evidence for certainty is not easy to come by. You might be certain that you have two hands by looking at them and showing them, as Moore proposes. But this is evidence of your being certain, not evidence of your having two hands (§250, 33). (Similarly, you might be certain of the existence of your foot, but this certainty manifests itself in your acting certain that you have a foot [§360, 47].) In considering the case of people who do not disbelieve but rather withhold certainty, even about things like whether water boils or freezes when held over a flame, Wittgenstein asks, 'What difference does this make in their lives? Isn't it just that they talk rather more about certain things than the rest of us?' (§338, 43). He even talks of the possibility of expressing 'comfortable certainty' as opposed to 'the certainty that is still struggling' (§357, 46). Having said enough about Wittgenstein's direct handling of certainty and doubt to have extracted the second methodological protocol (and previewed the third) for our Cultural Studies as the study of culture as ordering, we continue our trawling by considering some of his propositions about knowing, learning and judging.

Knowing, learning and judging within the limits of doubt and certainty

Wittgenstein tells us that the concept '"know" is analogous to the concepts "believe", "surmise", "doubt", "be convinced"', particularly as it is used in Moore's account. As such, assurances from reliable people that they know such and such are worthless (§21, 5). Consider, as an example, the proposition that no one has been on the moon (one Wittgenstein uses several times – in the late 1940s/early 1950s, well before it was a practical possibility). Wittgenstein says, 'Not merely is nothing of the sort ever seriously reported to us by reasonable people, but our whole system of physics forbids us to believe it.' He adds that if we were asked for directions to the moon, 'We should feel ourselves intellectually very distant from someone who said this' (§108, 17). This is a vaguely Pyrrhonian formulation; only the possible role given to physics suggests the possibility of knowledge beyond evident propositions.

Wittgenstein's (latent?) Pyrrhonism is further evident in his claim that statements by people that they know such-and-such are not interesting in themselves, but are interesting because of their 'role in the system of our empirical judgements' (§§137–8, 20–1). Similarly, he says, 'Whether I *know* something depends on whether the evidence backs me up or contradicts me. For to say one knows one has a pain means nothing' (§504, 66). For our trawling exercise, we read these remarks as further support for Protocol Two of our methodological approach: thinking, including doubt and certainty, forms definite, and hence describable, systems – inasmuch as it slightly extends this protocol: thinking, including doubt and certainty, and including those occasions where it is gathered into what is called knowledge, forms definite, and hence describable, systems.

Clearly there is also an element here of Wittgenstein's determination that we should always be looking at contexts of acting and behaving. We cannot, that is, dodge the constraint of context in order to 'know' in some pure way. When we stand up, for example, Wittgenstein reminds us, we don't need to know why we have two feet. 'There is no why. . . . This is how I act' (§148, 22). He adds later that the effect of saying 'I know' can be had without actually saying the words, that is, we believe certain things (where we are, having hands and feet, etc.) on the basis of us acting out those beliefs (§§427–8, 55). This is even more important where the words 'I know' carry some special significance, for instance in a court of law. In a court, a statement by a witness that 'I know' is insufficient, Wittgenstein argues. It must be shown that the witness was in a position to know. The circumstances of claims to know are crucial for their effectiveness (§441, 57).

In that there is no way for 'knowing' to find a way around the limits of systems and the contexts of acting and behaving, there is no point turning to 'experience' or 'truth' in the hope of finding such a way. For example, Wittgenstein argues that empirical knowledge, such as the knowledge that one will be dead if one's head is cut off, does not come from experience in isolation. Experience teaches us such empirical knowledge, but only as part of a set of interdependent propositions. In isolation we might doubt such knowledge as we have no direct experience of it (§274, 35). In other words, it is not experience *per se* that directs our knowledge, it is a system – a set of interdependent propositions. Wittgenstein says we 'acquire' such systems 'by means of observation and instruction'. It is the system that helps our beliefs hang together. He gives the example of someone who believes that cars grow out of the earth; such a person might not believe any of our propositions because he or she probably 'does not accept our whole system of verification' (§279, 36).

Truth is equally a dead-end. Wittgenstein asks, what does it mean to say that the truth of a proposition is certain (§193, 27)? In answering, he tells us that the 'use of the expression "true or false" has something misleading about it'. It 'is like saying "it tallies with the facts or it doesn't", and the very thing that is in question is what "tallying" is here'. 'Really "The proposition is either true or false" only means that it must be possible to decide for or against it. But this does not say what the ground for such a decision is like' (§§199–200, 27). In other words, context rears its head and truth cannot somehow get to us directly. Wittgenstein puts this point a slightly different way when he says that statements in the form of 'I know' are not presumptuous within the language-games in which they occur. Within the restricted setting of each game such statements hold a high position. Outside the context of the games in which they occur, they may appear false, but within these contexts they are so powerful that 'God himself can't say anything to me about them' (§554, 73).

The points we have made about Wittgenstein's sceptical approach to the activity we call 'knowing' can be concluded by our mentioning briefly what Wittgenstein says about knowing a colour. At its simplest, Wittgenstein suggests, knowing a colour might involve knowing the word for it in a particular language (§§530–1, 70). But this can quickly become complex: to say that a child knows the colour blue, for example, is to say something complex – along the lines of the child knowing English words (§§544–6, 71–2). This discussion of colours is a good point to turn to Wittgenstein's discussions of the activity of learning.

By now Wittgenstein's important moves in *On Certainty* should be familiar to you. We are, at this stage, consolidating and extending what we have called Protocols One and Two of our methodological approach and working towards Protocol Three, which we already know to be about context, acting and behaviours. This pattern informs what we have to report about Wittgenstein's remarks on both learning and judging. So, when he asks a complex question about learning and tries to bowl us over with a devastatingly simple answer – 'What is "learning a rule"? – *This*' (§28, 6) – we can keep our feet, understanding his claim as a sceptical move towards the notion of context, or the way something is actually used in practice. We are to have no truck, then, with the idea that rules somehow provide a bedrock for learning. Rules for learning, he tells us, have to be supported by practice (§139, 21). Furthermore, 'We do not learn the practice of making empirical judgements by learning rules: we are taught *judgements* and their connexion with other judgements' (§140, 21). Wittgenstein takes these points even further in arguing that children don't learn of the existence of objects like books by direct questions; they learn by being shown, by being asked to get a book, etc., which does not necessarily involve knowledge and doubt. He goes on, 'Does a child believe that milk exists? Or does it know that milk exists? Does a cat know that a mouse exists?' (§§476–8, 62–3). In arithmetic the fact that $12 \times 12 = 144$, for example, is not learnt

> through a rule, but by learning to calculate. . . . We got to know the *nature* of a rule by learning to calculate. . . . [We can even describe] how we satisfy ourselves of the reliability of a calculation . . . [without the use of a rule or without a rule emerging] . . . *This* is how one calculates. Calculating is *this*. What we learnt at school, for example. Forget this transcendent certainty, which is connected with your concept of spirit. . . . But remember: even when the calculation is something fixed for me, this is only a decision for a practical purpose. . . . When does one say, I know that [something] × [something] = [something]? When one has checked the calculation. (§§43–50, 8, original parenthesis)

Similarly, when Wittgenstein tells us that children learning to speak do not understand 'the concept *is called*' (§536, 71), we can guess where he is heading. He takes us there with the greatest precision in discussing children learning colours: 'A child must learn the use of colour words before it can ask for the name of a colour' (§548, 72). Furthermore, for a child to learn a language he or she must learn to identify colours – 'to attach the name of its colour to a white, black, red or blue object without the occurrence of any *doubt*' (§522, 68–9). Children learn colours to the point where they can say they know colours: 'And one child . . . will say, of another or of himself, that he already knows what such-and-such is called' (§§527–9, 70). It is in this way that language-games grow – they can be expanded by learning new words, as when children learn new colour words, or new words for a game about building with rocks, for instance (§566, 74–5).

It is by use or practice that learning takes place, just as for knowing, and just as for judging – 'My judgements themselves characterize the way I judge, characterize the nature of judgement' (§149, 22). So, when considering judgements about colours or hands or some other simple proposition, 'somewhere I must begin with not-doubting; and that is not, so to speak, hasty but excusable: it is part of judging' (§150, 22). It should almost go without saying that experience is not, for Wittgenstein, of itself sufficient as a basis for judgement. It has to be supported by other judgements, such as that which allows us to trust someone's or our own experience (§34, 56–7). But this is not to say that experience has no role to play in our judging. In learning to trust our judgements of evidence, we rely on experience. In a law court the evidence provided by a physicist that water boils at about 100 degrees centigrade is accepted unconditionally, as true, because of this trust in experience (§§603–4, 79–80).

Before we move on to the next section, in which we take the steps to extend Protocol Three, we summarise the steps we have taken in this section in regard to the present form of all three protocols. Here are the protocols in their first set of clothes:

- Protocol One: describe how things (including cultural objects and practices) appear.
- Protocol Two: thinking, including doubt and certainty, forms definite, and hence describable, systems.
- Protocol Three: in describing how things appear, we should be aware that appearances appear in contexts.

And here is how we have expanded Protocols One and Two:

- Protocol One: describe how things (including cultural objects and practices) appear and in doing so be careful not to rush to an explanation of the things.
- Protocol Two: thinking, including doubt and certainty, and including those occasions where it is gathered into what is called knowledge, forms definite, and hence describable, systems.

Already the protocols are beginning to grow large with methodological complexity. Please remember that after we rework Protocol Three and after we extend each protocol through a consideration of Law's contribution to our methodological discussion, in the conclusion to the chapter we render all the protocols into their most direct, very trim forms.

Use and practice as methodological devices

All the moves of Wittgenstein we relate in this section have been introduced. We have already seen his commitment to the notion of context.
Sometimes he directly uses the term 'context', sometimes he spells out a
context of action, behaviour and/or practice, rather than using the term
directly, and, as we see below, on occasion he uses 'circumstances' as a
synonym for 'context'. We suggest that it is feasible to work towards a
notion of *use* as an umbrella notion for what is being achieved by these
Wittgensteinian moves. So, we extend Protocol Three using a pot-pourri
of Wittgenstein's terms – in describing how things appear, we should be
aware that appearances appear in contexts, and in being so aware, we
should be aware that contexts involve actions, behaviours, uses, practice
and circumstances.

At this point it is appropriate that we acknowledge the important criticisms of Wittgenstein posed by Ernest Gellner in his *Language and
Solitude* (1998). Gellner sees the extreme atomism of the early
Wittgenstein and the extreme communalism of the later Wittgenstein
(*On Certainty* definitely belongs to this camp) as two aspects of the one
intellectual spectrum. In criticising both extremes for being too immod-
erate, for each not allowing any room for the other, Gellner treats
Wittgenstein's commitment to the notion of use as a communalist
extreme that shuts out the possibility of sensibly assessing the complex
production of knowledge at the end of the twentieth century. Our reading of Wittgenstein's thought attempts to side-step this criticism by
stressing its Pyrrhonian possibilities; our Wittgenstein is a Wittgenstein
of a limited method; the question of whether he is useful in assessing
knowledge production simply does not arise.

Let us examine some more of Wittgenstein's propositions that deal
with the notion of context (and its synonyms). He links reasonableness
to context – in a certain circumstance a 'reasonable person' might doubt
such and such (§334, 42). He describes certain aspects of court procedure in terms of context – a law court relies on circumstances to give
statements a 'certain probability' (§335, 42). And, more famously, he
discusses meanings in terms of context: for instance, he tells us that the
'words "I am here" have a meaning only in certain contexts . . . because
their meaning is not *determined* by the situation, yet stands in need of
such determination'. He adds, after considering the example of a dispute

about when one can be sure another is expressing certainty about recognising something, 'how a sentence is *meant* can be expressed by an expansion of it and may therefore be made part of it' (§348–9, 44–5). Obviously context has much work to do in Wittgenstein's philosophy. He offers the example of a man crying out bizarre words for no easily discernible reason and suggests we would make no sense of these words without context. He also offers the example of hand movements that suggest sawing and asks, 'but would one have any right to call this movement *sawing*, out of all context?' (§350, 45). He tells us that the statement 'I know I am in England' makes perfect sense in certain circumstances, but in others it is 'fishy' (§423, 54). Philosophers are not, of course, a special case: if a philosopher is to say something philosophical about a statement (say a statement about the existence of a tree), he or she has to specify the circumstances in which the statement is made (§433, 56). Needless to say, Moore is a special target – while Wittgenstein concedes that much of Moore's certainty about his 'I know' statements is well founded, he adds quickly that this is only so because of the context of these statements; different contexts could undermine this certainty (§622, 82).

Wittgenstein relies on the notion of context in developing the role of language-games. He stresses that different language-games have different contexts, concentrating his fire on the use of 'I know' claims. 'If someone says he *knows* something, it must be something that, by general consent, he is in a position to know' (§555, 73). For example, 'It is part of the language-game with people's names that everyone knows his name with the greatest certainty' (§579, 76). It is context, then, that makes sense of these two of Wittgenstein's claims:

> When language-games change, then there is a change in concepts, and with the concepts the meanings of words change. (§65, 10)

> I did not get my picture of the world by satisfying myself of its correctness; nor do I have it because I am satisfied of its correctness. . . . The propositions of this world-picture might be part of a kind of mythology. And their role is like that of rules of a game; and the game can be learned purely practically, without learning any explicit rules. (§§94–5, 15)

We are now in a position to close in on the centrality of the notion of use. In doing so, we should note, as we have hinted above, that use for Wittgenstein always entails calculation, in its broadest sense. That calculation for him always entails assumption and decision – even our calculations must begin with assumptions or decisions (§146, 22) – adds to our picture of the centrality of use, in that while use entails calculation, calculation entails the use of decisions and assumptions, which themselves are only justified by use (everything in our Wittgensteinian methodology keeps coming back to use). He makes his strongest point about calculations in demonstrating the futility of doubting them: to suppose that all calculations are in error might be crazy, but we cannot be certain that it is wrong; the only way we can be certain is via calculations; we rely on calculations (§217, 29).

Wittgenstein gives us a fairly straightforward example of the centrality of the notion of use in discussing the statement 'I can't be making a mistake.' He says this statement can only be justified 'in its everyday use' (§638, 84). He expands on this with a pointed anecdote. He tells of a strolling conversation with a friend in which he spoke of the attributes of elms, passed an ash and said 'See what I mean?' When his interlocutor told him the tree was an ash, he replied, 'I always meant ash when I said elm.' He says this is a perfectly legitimate way to eliminate mistakes and adds that this is how they are eliminated in calculations (§§649–50, 86).

We have already seen the way Wittgenstein advances his propositions about use by showing that colours have no basis except in the way they are used. The basis of all appearances, in his hands, is shaken such that it must be seen ultimately as a question of use. He even argues that the only thing against supposing that chairs and other apparent objects disappear or change shape when we are not looking at them and then reappear or change back when we look again is only that no one usually does suppose it (§214, 29); that is, such a supposition has no force because it is not used. Our learning, our knowing, our judging, our believing, our certainty, our doubt are all based on our doing, on our actions and behaviour, that is, on our *use*. Our methodological protocols lead to use.

We now turn again to John Law's (1994) *Organizing Modernity*, to the more directly methodological aspects of his ground-breaking work on the notion of ordering. In doing so, we aim to bring the three methodological protocols we have established into contact with the points about ordering which make up the bulk of the previous chapter. That is, we intend to use Law to feed the three protocols more rich food before we trim them down dramatically.

Law's methodological contribution

As we saw in Chapter 2, Law, strongly influenced by the work of Latour and Callon (for a discussion of some of the methodological implications of their work, see Kendall and Wickham 1999: chs 3–4), offers quite a few useful discussions about how one might study ordering. We summarise his discussions of: actor-network theory; relational materialism; reflexivity; symmetry; representations; non-reduction; and what he calls recursive process. We assess each one in terms of building up our three methodological protocols.

One of Law's first steps in advocating actor-network theory is to urge us to consider the ordering of intellectual ordering devices for studying ordering. Tricky, but worth following, if you dare. He thinks of actor-network theory as a framework built of 'many semiotic systems, many orderings, jostling together to generate the social'. This framework, according to Law, 'tends to tell *stories*, stories that have to do with the processes of ordering', processes that generate effects – 'technologies, stories about how actor-networks elaborate themselves, and stories which erode . . . the distinction between the macro and the micro-social' (1994: 18). He draws up a list of actor-network theory's potential objects of analysis – 'people, devices, texts, "decisions", organizations and interorganizational relations'. For Law, any analysis of modes of ordering must 'tell stories about these materials'. Such materials are 'social', but in the particular way in which actor-network theory understands this term (p. 23). As he explains this point he gives us something of a preview of his commitment to the notion of symmetry. The social world, for actor-network theory, Law tells us, is 'materially heterogeneous', meaning, in simple terms, that the above list must be seen to include 'machines, animals or architectures' as well as human beings. After arguing that social theory's traditional incapacity to take this step has been overcome to a limited extent by 'labour process theory, and some parts of feminism, which are deeply concerned with the relationships between technologies and social relations', Law turns to a point he says is still untouched by even these improvements – 'that the *differences* between materials may themselves be a series of (more or less precarious) effects' (p. 23).

This discussion can be said to add sensibly to Protocol One, at least for the purposes of studying cultural objects and practices. It will be recalled that in Chapter 1 we established the wisdom of accepting as the proper objects of Cultural Studies all objects and practices that have come to be so accepted (something which can now be seen as a decidedly Pyrrhonian/Wittgensteinian move). As such, in this chapter we have casually built this 'wisdom' into Protocol One as a parenthetical insert – describe how things (including cultural objects and practices) appear and in doing so be careful not to rush to an explanation of the things. To offer a full rendition of this protocol such that it incorporates the points Law makes here is to build it up considerably (into a very clumsy formulation): describe appearances and in describing the appearances of cultural objects and practices (and in being careful not to rush to an explanation of the things), be sure to include all features of actors and their networks – machines, people, devices, texts, decisions, organisations and inter-organisational relations.

Law expands this intervention by developing the notion of 'relational materialism' to serve alongside actor-network theory. He has two explicit reasons for so doing:

> The first has to do with social ordering itself, and is easily stated: there would be no social ordering if the materials which generate these were not heterogeneous. . . . For orderings spread, or (sometimes) seek to spread, across time and space. But, and this is the problem, left to their own devices human actions and words do not spread very far at all. For me the conclusion is inescapable. Other materials, such as texts and technologies, surely form a crucial part of any ordering. . . . So ordering has to do with both humans and non-humans. So it doesn't make much sense to ignore materials. And . . . it doesn't make too much sense to treat them separately, as if they were different in kind. (1994: 23–4, emphases removed)

This point is important for our project (in the way Law's handling of actor-network theory is important, as we discuss in more detail in the next section), but it needs to be accompanied by his modification of it: 'we need to include *all* materials in . . . analysis if we want to make sense of social ordering, but, symmetrically, I also take it that materials are better treated as products or effects rather than as having properties that are given in the order of things' (p. 24).

Law's second explicit reason for his advocacy of 'relational materialism' follows closely from his first. In thinking through the relationships between humans and non-humans, we have to be aware of the extent to which we, as analysts of ordering, have a role in producing the very categories themselves. While, he says, we cannot decide that a machine is a human being and vice versa, closer to the boundary between them our role as analysts is much more active: 'the issue becomes one of setting boundaries, of labelling. It becomes one of deciding how it is that we distinguish, for instance, between people (or "types" of people) on the one hand, and organizations or machines such as computers on the other' (p. 24).

As we say, we discuss Law's 'first reason' for supporting 'relational materialism' in the next section, when we undertake the radical dieting exercise. His 'second reason' for using it – that which heads us down the path of reflexivity – marks the beginning of a useful addition to Protocol Three – describe the uses of appearances. We say more about this after an extended discussion of his treatment of reflexivity.

Reflexivity, Law tells us in defining mode, 'may be seen as the extension of the principle of symmetry: in effect it says, there is no reason to suppose that we are different to those whom we study. We too are products' (p. 16). Reflexivity, in Law's hands, is a sort of alarm clock that rings to remind us that 'if we are engaged in the study of ordering, then we should, if we are to be consistent, be asking how it is that we came to (try to) order in the way that we did' (p. 17). Sagely, Law suggests that 'to lay down principles about reflexivity is surely self-defeating'. Yet he also notes, even more cleverly, that in engaging in investigation, in 'telling stories about the world', we are forced to 'say how things are', which is of course to lay down principles in some way. He calls this a 'nice dilemma' (p. 17). Law is sensible enough to avoid a grand answer to this dilemma, saying instead that, 'Provisionally, very provisionally, I tend towards the camp of the modest legislators, rather than the interpreters.' This means, he goes on, that he is prepared to report his observations of life in the laboratory he studied for his book – that is, his reflexivity does not go so far as to undermine his basic descriptive task – but feels compelled to report at the same time 'some of the contingencies and uncertainties – ethnographic, theoretical, personal and political – with which I have wrestled along the way' (p. 17). Law is adamant that we need to be modest as we go about our ordering. 'When we write about ordering there is no question of standing apart and observing from a distance. We're participating in ordering too. We're unavoidably involved in the modern reflexive project of monitoring, sensemaking and control' (p. 2). In other words, Law personally faces up to a basic research question: how should we handle the fact that we are just as caught up in ordering as are the things and people we write about (p. 2)? It should be clear that at the heart of his answer is an equally direct personal statement: by straightforward honesty. He says that while his book is a report of a year's fieldwork – an ethnographic study of the organisation of a large laboratory – this is only one of the stories he must tell (p. 2). Woven into this story are: a story about others, both the subjects in the laboratory and social theorists, and what they have to say about ordering; a story about wider politics and how the contests that inform them have an impact on the ordering of the laboratory and the ordering of many lives within it; and, crucially, a 'personal story', a story, by John Law and for John Law, of how he himself reacted to the stories of the people in the laboratory and of how he himself lived and acted as an ethnographer (pp. 3–4) (for a fascinating fuller treatment of the twists, turns and pitfalls involved in discussing reflexivity, see Cooper 1997).

Here is what all this means for Protocol Three – it now reads: describe the uses of appearances, including the use of describing the uses, and including the use involved in this last act of description, and including the use involved in this last act of description, and so on.

Law explains that symmetry is fundamentally about approaching everything one investigates in the same way (pp. 9–10). The advantages so gained include avoiding 'privileging anything or anyone' before you even start and avoiding the assumption that some phenomena do not need to be investigated. Investigators who adopt symmetry include within the scope of their investigations the process whereby some knowledge is judged true and other knowledge false, ensuring that this process does not quietly sneak away from the scene and avoid interrogation, as it so often seems to. Symmetry is yet another of Law's devices for overcoming the distinction between humans and non-humans (something of an obsession for him and something that we feel could usefully become an obsession for Cultural Studies). He suggests that to use symmetry in this task is necessarily to conduct an inquiry into what human agency means, how it is made what it is claimed to be (pp. 10–11). He summarises his approach to symmetry thus:

> [T]he principle of symmetry suggests that there is no privilege – that every-thing can be analysed and that it can (and should) be analysed in the same terms. . . . [T]he principle of symmetry is simply a methodological restate-ment of the relationship between order and ordering. It says, in effect, that

we shouldn't take orders at face value. Rather we should treat them as the outcome of ordering. (Law 1994: 12)

This is indeed a useful addition to our protocols, not for its repetition of the humans/non-humans theme, which we deal with later, but for the way it encourages investigators to include all pieces of knowledge – whether they have been previously labelled true or false, or even if they have not been so classified – into the scope of their investigations. For those studying cultural objects and practices, Protocol Two – which currently reads 'thinking, including doubt and certainty, and including those occasions where it is gathered into what is called knowledge, forms definite, and hence describable, systems' – needs to be understood to include all knowledge about the object or practice under investigation, no matter what system is used to order it. For example, when investigating television viewing practices, a thorough investigation (or set of investigations; obviously no single investigation can cover everything) will include thorough investigation of religious systems of classifying television content that work to prescribe (and proscribe) viewing possibilities in some countries or regions, thorough investigation of less formal systems that circulate among parents to the same end (though of course with very different rationales), and even thorough investigation of systems of thinking and knowledge based on astrology, or other such knowledge endeavours, that serve to restrict, or at least guide, viewing practices, as well as thorough investigation of the systems assumed by standard social science or industry surveys of viewing practices.

So we can expand Protocol Two as follows: thinking, including doubt and certainty, and including those occasions where it is gathered into what is called knowledge, forms definite, and hence describable, systems (and these systems order the knowledge into many forms, not simply those called 'true').

In discussing representation, Law says that ordering 'depends on representation' – 'representations shape, influence and participate in ordering practices' (p. 25, emphasis removed). Here, Law is not talking about representations of fixed interests, as in some cruder Marxist and Weberian accounts, which he sees as too 'Whiggish', 'functionalist' and 'limited'. In acknowledging that representations 'are not just part of ordering', and that they 'are ordering processes in their own right' (pp. 25–6, emphases removed), he urges us to abandon any 'correspondence theory of representation'. He wants us to recognise that what is important about a representation is its 'workability or legitimacy', not 'whether it corresponds to reality' (p. 26, emphasis removed).

Law is especially concerned that we recognise

> the way in which heterogeneous materials combine to tell, embody and perform a series of ordering modes and, as such, operate to generate reflexive and ordering places, those that are cloistered and are set aside. I'm concerned then with the material gradients and arrangements that strain towards the western ideal of pure consciousness, of perfect decision making. Or, to put it slightly differently, I'm concerned with the way in which material efforts generate the illusion of mind–body dualism – a dualism in which the mind masters the body. (p. 26)

At this stage, we can summarise this intervention as another addition to Protocol Two. Protocol Two now reads (we emphasise the new words): thinking, including doubt and certainty, and including those occasions where it is gathered into what is called knowledge, *making use of representations*, forms definite, and hence describable, systems (and these systems, *making use of representations*, order the knowledge into many forms, not simply those called 'true').

Law's treatment of non-reduction – a 'component' in his 'modest sociology' – acknowledges the authority of stories of reduction. Based on the requirement that knowledge endeavours attempt 'to explain a great deal on the basis of a few principles', such stories 'are the dominant mode of Western rationalist story-telling', with the capacity to 'convert the stories that they tell into principles' (p. 12). In trying to break down this authority, Law uses the example of a reductionist story in social theory that collapsed in on itself when pushed to its limits: he briefly recounts at least part of the history of Marxism in the twentieth century as a history of the demise of a deterministic story. This story, in which the 'superstructure' – politics and culture, including law – was determined by the economy, by the 'social relations of production', lost its credibility and had to be supplemented by another story. This supplementary story, authored largely by Althusser, rewrote the original ending, such that determination by the economy was allowed a dignified exit – it was now said to be deterministic only in 'the last instance', an instance that famously never comes (pp. 12–13). Law is surprisingly deferential to this supplementary story. He eventually dumps it, but along the way he uses it to make some important points:

I think there's an interesting tension in Althusser's stance. On the one hand, he was trying to save something from the wreckage of classical Marxism. . . . Thus classical Marxism took a fairly straightforward explanatory form, explaining *why* it is that superstructures take the form that they do . . . Althusser's rescue attempt – an attempt to come to terms with the complexities of ordering – made use of the relational but synchronic explanatory apparatus developed in structuralism. For structuralism is all about *relations*. It is a way of describing *how* it is that effects . . . are generated as a function of their location in a set of relations. So in structuralism there are 'hows', but there are none of the 'whys' preferred by reductionist Marxism. Structuralism describes: it does not explain: it isn't much good at telling stories with beginnings, middles and ends. It lives in the present. Or better, it is out of time altogether. And this is why terms such as 'in the last instance', which attempt to tell us 'why' stories in a 'how' vocabulary, don't really add up to much. (1994: 13)

This set of remarks from Law can be expressed as three, slightly different, parenthetic inserts, one at the end of each protocol:

- Protocol One: describe appearances and in describing the appearances of cultural objects and practices (and in being careful not to rush to an explanation of the things), be sure to include all features of actors and their networks – machines, people, devices, texts, decisions, organisations and inter-organisational relations (it should be remembered that we are interested only in how the appearances appear, not in why they appear).
- Protocol Two: thinking, including doubt and certainty, and including those occasions where it is gathered into what is called knowledge, making use of representations, forms definite, and hence describable, systems (and these systems, making use of representations, order the knowledge into many forms, not simply those called 'true') (it should be remembered that we are interested only in how the thinking is gathered and forms systems, not in why it is and does).
- Protocol Three: in describing how things appear, we should be aware that appearances appear in contexts, and in being so aware, we should be aware that contexts involve actions, behaviours, uses, practice and circumstances *and* we should be aware that to describe the uses of appearances must include describing the use of describing the uses, and include describing the use involved in this last act of description, and include describing the use involved in this last act of description, and so on (it should be remembered that we are interested only in how the appearances are used, not in why they are used).

Law works up to his intervention about 'recursive process' by stating that he aims for investigations that, in being 'modest', are 'relational, with no privileged places, no dualisms and no a priori reductions'. These are to be, he says, investigations that do not 'distinguish between those that drive and those that are driven', although, he adds hastily, 'a relative distinction between the drivers and the driven, may *emerge* and be sustained' (p. 13). He summarises thus:

> [W]e tell stories, offer metaphorical redescriptions, ethnographies . . . which suggest that some effects are generated in a more rather than less stable manner, stories which explore how it is that divisions that look like dualisms come to look that way . . . [as well as stories] about patterns in the generative relationships, regularities which might be imputed, places where the patterns seem to reproduce themselves. (1994: 14)

'Recursive process', he tells us after this lead-up work, is another device for drawing our attention to the need to see things in terms of verbs, to emphasise actions. He is, in this context and in general, particularly drawn to the traditions of what are loosely called 'interpretive sociologies' (symbolic interactionism, ethnomethodology, and so on; sometimes these approaches are known by the term 'qualitative') because of their commitment to action through interaction (pp. 14–15). He recognises that his 'verb-centred' approach must 'slip up from time to time, for it is difficult to tug away from the dualism of nouns', but even so, he says, this is the 'simpler part of the message about process' (p. 15).

The more complex part, he tells us, has to do with '*recursion*', with what '*drives* social processes' (p. 15). Having foregone the opportunity to look 'outside' for the driving force – that would be reductionist – Law admits that 'we're left with this awkward conclusion: somehow or other, they are driving themselves'. He adapts Giddens to add that 'the social is both a medium and an outcome' (p. 15). The 'process' part of this formulation of Law can be added easily to Protocol One (again we use the technique of emphasising the new words): describe appearances and in describing the appearances of *the activities that make up* cultural objects and practices (and in being careful not to rush to an explanation of the things), be sure to include all features of actors and their networks – machines, people, devices, texts, decisions, organisations and inter-organisational relations (it should be remembered that we are interested only in how the appearances appear, not in why they appear).

Law's notion of 'recursion' is slightly trickier. Yet, even remembering that at the heart of this chapter, indeed, at the heart of this book, is the proposition that cultural objects and practices (what it is that the practitioners of Cultural Studies actually study) are both means of ordering people's lives *and*, at the same time, markers of that ordering – in other words, culture is both a medium and an outcome of ordering – we believe we can render our protocols thoroughly 'recursed' by employing another small addition to Protocol One:

- Protocol One: describe appearances and in describing the appearances of the activities that make up cultural objects and practices *and those that are made up by them* (and in being careful not to rush to an explanation of the things), be sure to include all features of actors and their networks – machines, people, devices, texts, decisions, organisations and inter-organisational relations (it should be remembered that we are interested only in how the appearances appear, not in why they appear).

That's as full as our three protocols are going to get. Now it is time for us to reduce them into a more manageable and pithy form.

Conclusion: the short form of the three protocols

Our final task for the chapter is to slim our three methodological protocols down to their most direct form. If you think we are saying that all the complex and sometime convoluted propositions we've put to you up to this point can be summed up in a few simple lines, you are right. We think it is important that you can navigate your way through the twists and turns we have had to travel to get to these points, and even to exercise the dietary technique at the core of this section on your own thinking, but if you disagree, then we suppose you will boil the chapter down to the three protocols you will find facing you shortly and go on your way.

The first step in our radical diet is the 'full and frank examination' step. Here are the three protocols at their largest and most unwieldy:

- Protocol One: describe appearances and in describing the appearances of the activities that make up cultural objects and practices and those that are made up by them (and in being careful not to rush to an explanation of the things), be sure to include all features of actors and their networks – machines, people, devices, texts, decisions, organisations and inter-organisational relations (it should be remembered that we are interested only in how the appearances appear, not in why they appear).

- Protocol Two: thinking, including doubt and certainty, and including those occasions where it is gathered into what is called knowledge, making use of representations, forms definite, and hence describable, systems (and these systems, making use of representations, order the knowledge into many forms, not simply those called 'true') (it should be remembered that we are interested only in how the thinking is gathered and forms systems, not in why it does).

- Protocol Three: in describing how things appear, we should be aware that appearances appear in contexts, and in being so aware, we should be aware that contexts involve actions, behaviours, uses, practice and circumstances and we should be aware that to describe the uses of appearances must include describing the use of describing the uses, and include describing the use involved in this last act of description, and include describing the use involved in this last act of description, and so on (it should be remembered that we are interested only in how the appearances are used, not in why they are used).

We'll strip back Protocol One first. In regard to the additions to this protocol based on Law's points about actor-network theory, we feel confident that the phrase 'describe appearances' can be read by those who are actually doing the studying of particular cultural objects and practices to include both 'describe how things (including cultural objects and practices) appear' and 'in describing the appearances of cultural objects and practices, be sure to include all features of actors and their networks – machines, people, devices, texts, decisions, organisations and inter-organisational relations'. If it cannot be so read, then the objects and practices under investigation are not 'appearances' and as such can play no part in the Cultural Studies we are advocating. We remain confident that it can and will be read in this way and note, again, that Law worries a little too much.

In assessing what we presented about Law's 'relational materialism', we suggest that our summary offers more evidence for the point made immediately above. While we should think of Protocol One in terms of describing the appearances of things without making a distinction between the humans and non-humans, we should only do so up to the point where our focus is still clearly on *appearances*. If we find ourselves having to employ complex justifications, as Law sometimes does, then we have strayed too far from what we are supposed to be doing. In other words, with an eye to some of Collins's arguments against some of the 'treat humans and non-humans equally' formulations of Latour and Callon (see especially Collins and Yearley 1992), we take Law's 'modification' here to mean that while machines and other non-human materials must be taken into account when investigating ordering, they should not be taken to be special – in rejecting anthropomorphic accounts of ordering, we must be careful not to simply replace them with 'machineomorphic' accounts.

Now we turn our attention to Protocol Two. Law's discussion about representation clearly has important ontological and epistemological ramifications for our project (as our large version of Protocol Two amplifies), but we think we can take these ramifications on board without the baggage of a notion of representations. Law is correct to argue that 'representations shape, influence and participate in ordering practices', correct to reject the 'correspondence theory of representation' and correct to reject the mind–body dualism in favour of descriptions of how it is put in place by representations. He is on the right road; he just stops his journey before he should. Of course the objects of the study of ordering – in our case cultural objects and practices as ordering objects and practices – include various kinds of portrayals of things, and of course such a study of ordering does not require us to see the portrayals as corresponding to the things, especially not to see a special category of portraying called mind and a special category of things called body. But we have already seen that we can sensibly treat the portrayals as things – as objects themselves – and describe them carefully, as we would other things. So why bother with a notion of representation at all? It may have been a useful ladder Law used to climb to his position, but unless he intends to climb down at some point in the future, it is now, as far as the study of ordering is concerned, useless.

Now, to Protocol Three. We admire and endorse much of Law's account of reflexivity as a methodological tool, but we suggest that he is too personal in his approach. We have no quibble with his various 'stories' of the way he conducted his project in the laboratory – his honesty is praiseworthy, yet surely not as noteworthy as he suggests. Our three protocols, built from Pyrrhonism and Wittgenstein's *On Certainty*, assume and, we hope, reflect philosophical rigour. We are offering a set of methodological protocols for Cultural Studies as the study of ordering which, while vulnerable to personal dishonesty in the way intellectual production in general is vulnerable, does not focus on the personal level, but on the level of procedure. The core suggestion of Protocol Three – describe the uses of appearances – contains an operating procedure for Cultural Studies as the study of ordering. The type of reflexivity Law urges could not be built on to Protocol Three by the simple addition of a few words: describe the uses of appearances, including the use of describing the uses. No, to cash out Law's point in full we had to go with our very wordy formulation – we should be aware that to describe the uses of appearances must include describing the use of describing the uses, and include describing the use involved in this last act of description, and include describing the use involved in this last act of description, and so on – and as we did this, we knew we were bloating our third protocol.

Having now made the point that Law's reflexivity is too personal, we can quickly trim quite a lot from Protocol Three by limiting the amount of reflexivity involved in our methodological steps. While we endorse reflexivity as a methodological goal, we think it has to be kept in check, lest it become destructive. Our comments about Law's over-personal formulation suggest a concern on our part that this style of reflexivity is in some danger of collapsing into a confessional morass, whereby honest statements by honest researchers about their roles in their research projects and their feelings about their roles come to swamp the descriptions of appearances that are supposedly at the core of these projects. Of course, with our non-personal formulation, we too have to be wary of too much reflexivity: the prospect of studies of some cultural object or practice being lost in endless accounts by researchers of their involvement in the descriptive process is not a happy one. As such, we make ours a one-step reflexivity: describe the uses of appearances, including the first use of describing the uses.

Now we turn our attention to all three protocols at once. While we see no particular value in Law's detour into structuralism, it has to be said that the methodological preference for 'how' over 'why' that he draws from it is central to our project in this book, so we are hardly in a position to criticise him for milking structuralism in the way he does.

We do not put it the same way he does – we think our protocols, even in their most basic form, shunt 'why' out of the way in favour of 'how' – but this is not really a criticism. Just because we feel comfortable translating a lot of Law's methodological formulations into fewer and fewer words does not mean we are not grateful to him. Our gratitude to Law, we think, sits well alongside our (albeit deeper) gratitude to Pyrrhonism and to Wittgenstein. We trust our three sparse protocols are read as markers of our gratitude.

Here they are, three trim protocols we hope you will use to guide your study of culture as ordering, and which we try to cash out in the four chapters that follow:

- Protocol One: describe appearances.
- Protocol Two: describe the appearances of systems of thinking and knowledge.
- Protocol Three: describe the uses of appearances.

4 Ordering Through the Culture of Government – a Colonial Example

To talk of ordering through the culture of government is to do a lot of talking – it is a big topic. We must face it: it is too big for a single chapter in a book like this, a book that is aiming to introduce a new way of going about studying culture. A sub-category is needed, a more manageable example within the field of ordering by government. To this end we concentrate in this chapter on colonial government from the perspective of culture; more particularly we focus on the government of the early Australian colonies. We argue that this example of colonial government was actually conducted *through* culture.

Usually, of course, such political questions as colonialism and imperialism are analysed as if politics, or what we might call the macro-level, can supply all the answers. In such studies culture may be thought interesting, but it is usually relegated to an epiphenomenal or ideological level. However, a close examination of some aspects of the government of the Australian colonies by the British in the nineteenth century allows the argument that not only was the government of culture uppermost in the minds of the British, but in fact the Australian colonies were governed through culture, taste and civilisation.

Liberalism, administration, and techniques of the self

We think it is clear that this attempt to govern culture is much more characteristic of the liberal nineteenth century than of the eighteenth century. The British colonialism of the eighteenth century was, frankly, much less sophisticated from a cultural governance point of view. Colonialism was conducted in a primarily military framework and it was consequently the military (and of course commercial) benefits of colonial rule that were paramount. In the nineteenth century, all this changed as the British, under the impress of a liberal problematisation of rule, began to understand their empire as a *cultural* phenomenon.

Foucault (especially 1986b) has drawn our attention to the mutuality between governing others and governing our selves, especially as enunciated by the ancients (a theme to which we return in a later chapter). This mutuality is also a feature of the nineteenth century (whose administrators, as we shall see, were profoundly influenced by the antique tradition). In the nineteenth century, the conduct of rule became a matter of intense concern and reflection – for the British, this was not just a reflection on the techniques and forms of rule, it was also an inquisition into the ethical justification for rule. We see in this period, following Foucault, a shift from morals to ethics – from a simple, externally imposed system of rules for conduct, to an internal reflection on how to constitute oneself as a subject of one's own actions. The ethical dimension is about the construction of a relationship with oneself (the *rapport à soi*); the moral dimension concerns how the self simply obeys a code which is external to it and with which it does not engage in any dynamic and mutually transformatory relationship.

Particularly in *The Care of the Self*, Foucault (1986b) suggests that the West has a long tradition of assuming a set of connections between forms of government and mastery at a variety of levels, usually the self, the family and others. In a nutshell, it is not unusual for an intimate relationship between self-mastery and the mastery of others to be assumed and insisted upon: if you want to govern other people you must first learn to govern yourself. Now this theme of the relationship between the government of self and of others is very noticeable in the nineteenth-century liberal tradition. Liberalism is very insistent on the notion that government of others requires self-mastery. It is perhaps useful here to think of liberalism, not especially in terms of political philosophy or practice, but as the constant problematisation of government: liberalism contains within it the fear of over-governing, of governing too much. The liberal *rapport à soi*, then, is a means of establishing something like a moral authority to govern (for a fuller exposition of these ideas, in both general terms and with specific examples, see Barry et al. 1996; Osborne 1994; Rose 1990, 1999; Rose and Miller 1992).

Okay, but how did this actually translate into governmental action? Good question: we answer it by briefly examining the formation and operation of the 'administrative machineries' that established a flow of government between Britain and the Australian colonies – the civil or public service. The civil service was, of course, essentially bureaucratic in operation, a device which enabled government of others, while adhering to the premise that self-mastery and the mastery of others cannot be separated. It was this 'bureaucratisation' of Australia that was the crucial moment in the formation of certain sorts of self-regulating citizens. As Ian Hunter argues:

> the bureau . . . provides the ethical conditions for a special comportment of the person. The ethical attributes of the good bureaucrat – strict adherence to procedure, acceptance of sub- and super-ordination, esprit de corps, abnegation of personal moral enthusiasms, commitment to the purposes of the office . . . are a positive moral achievement requiring the mastery of a difficult ethical milieu and practice. (1994: 156–7)

The civil service in Britain changed rapidly in the nineteenth century. As we have already noted, in the eighteenth century British colonial policy was chiefly commercial and military. However, in the nineteenth century it became political and cultural. The emerging science of political economy, which took the health, wealth and happiness of the population as its object, really took off in the civil service. For example, William Huskisson, who was at the Colonial Office for just six months during the period 1827–28, made stringent efforts to reshape the ethos of colonialism: 'he defended Imperial preference on political rather than on economic grounds' (Morrell 1966: 4; see also Huskisson 1831).

This allowed a new way of ordering emigration: emigration began to be understood as something other than the weakening of the power of Britain. Flows of population were beginning to be theorised in much more complex ways than the previous world views, derived from cameralist philosophies, that held a reasonably simple equivalence between size of a nation's population and its power. The population's quality came to be seen as important – its productivity, its health, and so forth – but this quality was understood as a *cultural* as well as a political phenomenon. This shift in turn led to some interesting and quite strange

(strange to us) nexuses being built up in the nineteenth-century British bureaucratic culture. For example, there was a close link between political economy and the classics (politics *is* culture, and vice versa), which can be seen, for example, in the person of Herman Merivale, Professor of Political Economy at Oxford, a noted classicist, who was chosen to assume many of James Stephen's duties at the Colonial Office on his retirement in 1847. Stephen had virtually run the Colonial Office single-handedly and his retirement finally allowed the parcelling up of duties considered too much for one person. Yet Merivale's appointment demonstrates to us the importance attached to culture (as understood through a classical scholarly background) and the new science of political economy (see also Merivale 1861).

The well known bureaucrat Edward Gibbon Wakefield was the 'prophet of the new imperialism' (Morrell 1966: 5) in the British civil service. He made colonisation a branch of political economy at a time when the latter was held in the highest regard. However, it was becoming more and more obvious that government at a distance was an enormous challenge, and that it was necessary to think about new mechanisms for stopping Australia going the way of the USA. By 1840, for example, Charles Buller urged in regard to the position of Governor of New South Wales: 'he must carry on the government by and with the few officials whom he finds in possession when he arrives' (Buller 1840; cf. Morrell 1966: 17–26). The idea of forming a local civil service as an aid to responsible government was now an urgent requirement.

As early as 1827, a salaried civil service for New South Wales had been proposed. Much of the administration was about keeping and maintaining files on each inhabitant. Most of the administrators were convicts or emancipists until about 1855. This insertion of the convicts into the administrative functions which sought to tame the very same convicts was a very Benthamite solution. So, for example, a convict came up with the idea of the nightwatch. The complex social stratification which ensued undermined the possibility of a 'convict loyalty' (Davidson 1991).

James Stephen, who became Permanent Under-Secretary in the British Colonial Office in 1836, carried out an administrative revolution in relation to the governing of the Australian colonies. He insisted on extensive minuting of meetings and decisions and the routinisation of colonial administration. However, he developed a strictly hierarchical system which disallowed senior clerks from making decisions – everything had to be referred to the centre: him. Stephen wanted civil servants to be part of a routinised machine, with himself as the overseer.

Local civil services were gradually established in the Australian colonies, with Victoria leading the way. The Victorian Civil Service Act of 1862, which was loosely modelled on the Northcote-Trevelyan report in Britain, stipulated entrance into the service by competitive examination and promotion by merit. The recommendations of this report were that service in the colonial office necessitated a university education in Britain, although the Australians did not always follow this recommendation, already being somewhat anti-elitist. The deeper motive was the construction of a new cultural and administrative intelligentsia. The task was to shape a new cultural sensibility in government. As Peter Gowan puts it:

> the propertied classes must devote a part of their wealth to the enlightenment, cultivation and improvement of the people, tasks to be undertaken by forming a cadre of dedicated, cultured intellectuals imbued with a profound sense of duty. (Gowan 1987: 26)

> This [cadre or] clerisy could be constructed through the reformed universities, a new breed of civil servants and figures . . . in public life. . . . [T]here would be a new balance between the classes. (Gowan 1987: 29)

This new administrative elite, then, were well (and preferably university) educated, and selected according to merit – hence the virtually contemporaneous development of the public examination. The construction of the administrator as a self-aware individual was predicated on this notion of fair selection, which provided a justification for the rigours and responsibilities of governing. The new administrative elite was a meritocracy.

To sum up, we have made a few schematic remarks on the establishment of an administrative machinery in Britain and in and for Australia. You will already have a sense of the way in which the formation of the bureau is simultaneously the formation of a certain ethical mode of comportment of self. The bureaucrat is a specific moral personality. We now expand on this theme and talk more generally about 'fidelity techniques', or ways of establishing allegiance when one is governing at a distance.

Governing distant times and spaces: it's all Greek to some

Many of the techniques for establishing fidelity at a distance relate to attempts to mould the citizen body in a specific way (and see also Latour 1986, 1990; Law 1986; Osborne 1994). We have already referred, for example, to the way in which convicts were made part of a system of record keeping, which acted as a kind of reformatory principle by enclosing the convict within bureaucratic life. Many other techniques seem to stem from the nineteenth-century liberal obsession with antiquity and with the ancient world as a model for good practice. Many in the colonial office and in government were expert classicists and wrote works comparing the British Empire with the Greek or Roman (see, for example, Bryce 1914; Lucas 1912).

Jenkyns (1980) argues that much was made of similarities between ancient and British empires in the period which saw the flowering of liberalism. The Greeks represented the pinnacle of artistic and cultural achievement, while the Romans represented the best way to run an empire. The civilising mission of the Romans was also Britain's (Jenkyns 1980: 333). However, it seems to us that Jenkyns has missed the fact that the *cultural* role of imperialism became paramount and that, consequently, the Greek notion of colonisation was the one that was the most crucial for British colonists. Edward Freeman wished that all English-speakers had a noun to include them in the same family, as the Greeks had 'Hellene'. Seeley (1883), writing in the late nineteenth century, suggests that Greece was an unconscious influence on the colonial Briton.

Many colonial thinkers despaired of the situation in the colonies because they were not 'balanced' like Britain was thought to be 'balanced'. It was impossible to form 'decent' society, it was thought, without all the constituent cultural parts (including clergy, aristocracy, etc.). It was therefore increasingly important to have all classes of society represented in Australia. The models here were the Athenian colonies, which in supposedly being miniaturised copies of Athens, were to feel an affinity and a loyalty to the mother country which would not need to be enforced. Gladstone, who was strongly in favour of self-government, likened this to the Greek rather than the Roman method of empire, based on ties of sentiment and mutual benefit, allowing 'perfect freedom and perfect self-government' (cited in Macintyre 1991: 66).

What became especially evident was an attempt to make Australia as culturally like Britain as possible. This was a technical means of governing and ensuring a particular type of citizen with an ethical commitment to the empire. There were many examples of this tendency. In 1861, Edward Wilson set up the Acclimatisation Society to introduce, acclimatise and domesticate 'all innoxious animals, birds, fish, insects and vegetables, whether useful or ornamental'. In 1858, Edward Lytton, the Colonial Secretary of State, set up the colonial honours system, which explicitly set out to establish a kind of Australian aristocracy. This served the dual function of making the beneficiaries more faithful to Britain and making Australian society more balanced. Some aspects of life in the colonies were made more similar to their British counterparts. For example, where the colonial service uniform had been of a military cut, with lots of gold braid and plumage, in consultation with Prince Albert, Lytton now decreed that it would be the same as for civil servants in Britain (that is, grey, boring and functional).

Strenuous attempts were made to pull down and rebuild the architecture of the Australian cities and remodel them in Hellenic style. Both Light's Adelaide and Hoddle's Melbourne were set out according to a grid plan, in imitation of the classical colonial practice. This classical rationalisation of urban space had many consequences for utopian panoptic theorists; and, perhaps more prosaically, the parcelling up and selling of land was accomplished with ease from Britain. At the same time as the drill was breaking down the movements of convicts and soldiers into reliable and observable sub-routines, the grid was breaking the city down into an observable and calculable entity. The cultural space of the city was redesigned in a way which enabled facilitated ordering.

The nineteenth-century 'cult of Hellenism' provided Australians with a code of private manners and public conduct (oratorical styles, public architecture, etc.). Restraint, classical good taste, and so forth were counterposed to the gothic excess of many of the city churches. Hellenism was a way of providing oneself with good taste and it is interesting to note, as Paul de Serville (1980, 1991) does, that in the Melbourne of the 1850s, the civil service was regarded as an oasis of gentility, modesty and good taste amidst the vulgarity of the goldrush population.

As Sheldon Rothblatt (1976) argues, from the eighteenth century onwards 'civilisation' was an ethical term, marking a difference between Europeans and barbarians. It could be defined as the release from instinct, or the use of self-mastery. A classical, liberal education was seen as the best route to civilisation, and it was precisely this education which was given to civil servants in Britain and which formed a kind of ideal of pre-civil service education in Australia. The goal of a liberal education was 'taste'; it was not surprising, then, that there was a link between Hellenism, liberalism, and the civil service, especially as the latter was gradually being reformed as a training ground of good taste.

What we can see, from the middle of the nineteenth century, then, is a curious attempt to make Australia simultaneously British (or sometimes English rather than British) and Greek (Kendall 1997). Redmond Barry was a typical example of this tendency as he attempted to make Victoria a kind of Anglo-Greek hybrid, all the while despairing of his philistine fellow colonists, whom he privately called 'the Boeotian herd' (de Serville 1991: 245). Many Melbournians went hell for leather in pursuit of classical pieces with which to decorate their houses – most of the classical art treasures in Australia (and Australia still has a disproportionately large collection of antiquities and community of classical scholars for its size) made their way to Victoria, bought by goldrush money (de Serville 1980, 1991).

However, in terms of 'taste' as a way of forming the self as a (cultured) ethical subject, it is interesting that the ancient world was not the only resource for the Australian trying to establish himself or herself. In the nineteenth century the Australian colonies, like the motherland, experienced a more general cult of antiquarianism, fuelled by works such as Bernard Burke's *The General Armory* (1884) and his later *A Genealogical and Heraldic History of the Colonial Gentry* (1891 and 1895), which was an ever-increasing list of Coats of Arms and served as a kind of pattern-book, enabling people to produce personalised writing paper, cufflinks, silver, windows, tombstones, etc. All one had to do was look up one's surname, regardless of whether or not one was related to the armigerous family, and organise the necessary items from a burgeoning industry.

Returning to our analysis of the cult of Hellenism, we offer further discussion as to how it made the move from Britain to Australia and was there used to justify a faith in the 'motherland'. This cult, almost as soon as it arose in Britain early in the nineteenth century, became linked to practices of government in the Australian and other colonies. Briefly, the ancient Greeks provided colonial administrators with a variety of resources: not just codes of private and public manners (Macintyre 1991), but also a means of conceptualising the ethics of colonisation and, through close readings of ancient texts, a set of guidelines for handling practical situations (Ogilvie 1964). Hellenism, then, was not an interest in the Greeks for their theoretical value; it was an attempt to use the Greeks in a very practical way to formulate a set of techniques for everyday life (a theme to which we return in a later chapter; cf. Hadot 1995).

We stress that the British obsession with the ancient Greeks was, as we have already hinted and as Frank Turner emphasises, a nineteenth-century phenomenon. Until the end of the eighteenth century, the tendency was to regard European civilisation rather as Roman and, of course, Christian (Turner 1981: 81; Jenkyns 1980). At the beginning of the nineteenth century, however, the Greeks began to receive the attention previously given to the Romans. Suddenly, the Greeks were seen as more relevant, or at any rate as more similar to the British; more precisely, the Greeks provided 'a means for achieving self-knowledge and cultural self-confidence within the emerging order of liberal democracy and secularism' (Turner 1981: xii). This was primarily because the Romans were regarded as having a predominantly military empire – again, something we have already touched upon – while the Greek Empire was seen as an instrument of their civilising and cultural mission (for a later statement of a similar position, see Livingstone 1912). But while the main means of understanding the British Empire at the beginning of the nineteenth century was much more consonant with this reading of the Greeks than with any Roman equivalent, it was a reading that actually involved at least some rewriting of Greek history. Virtually all the eighteenth-century histories of Greece were anti-Athenian, and favourable to the overtly militaristic state of Sparta (see, for example, Gillies 1792), yet the nineteenth-century cult of Hellenism was a cult of Athenian Hellenism. The Athenian experience, then, was the one which was deemed to speak to the British concerned with problems of colonisation.

Virtually everyone who wrote about colonisation in the nineteenth century – popular, political or academic – had something to say about the contemporary relevance of antiquity. Most writers derogated the

Roman military system of running an empire and, in turn, praised the Greek model. So, for example, an anonymous speaker in Melbourne in 1861 claimed of the French:

> Their system of colonization resembles the Roman, their colonists are sol-diers, and the country becomes in their heads rather a military post than a commercial state. We resemble the Greeks. The Colonies which they founded in Asia Minor, Italy and Sicily rivalled the parent state in the cul-tivation of literature and art; their Government was free, but they still looked to the mother country for protection and assistance, and held them-selves under a very strong obligation to befriend and assist her in all her difficulties. (Anon 1861: 4)

John Dunmore Lang (1852) devoted a large section of his book on freedom and independence to an account of classical methods of colonisation. He noted how Roman colonisation was merely the estab-lishment of garrison towns, while the Greeks had a cultural mission. For Lang, as for so many others at the time, colonisation was a lost art; the British could regain their sense of how to practise the art of colonisation by looking at how the Greeks played their colonising role. Edward Freeman contrasted Athens and England, expressing his alarm at how England had become distanced from her colonies, espe-cially America, and he predicted the same fate for the British relationship with the Australian colonies. For Freeman, the root cause of these actual or impending colonial disasters was the fact that England and its colonies were not so united as Athens and its colonies had been (Stephens 1895: II, 180). In all of this, it is not difficult to see how colonisation practices were being rethought under the influence of liberal philosophy; but it was Hellenism that provided practical solutions which appealed to the liberal temper.

Many writers argued that the Australian colonies should be con-structed in such a way that they had within them all classes of society and suggested that problems in the colonies stemmed from the absence of the 'balance' discussed earlier as well as the consequent lack of an appropriate morale (see, for example, Wright 1847). Wakefield, instru-mental in establishing the colony that became South Australia, subscribed to this view, and along with influential commentators like Charles Buller and Bishop Hinds, suggested that successful colonisation depended on transplanting what he called 'the whole tree' of British society to Australia (see Wakefield 1914; Buller 1840; Parliamentary Papers 1850: xl (Cmd. 1163), 54ff.; Letter of FitzRoy to Grey

21/6/1849; CO 13/75: 22/3/1852; CO 13/79: 22/3/1852). Parliamentary debates on Australian immigration from the 1840s onward routinely deplored the 'low quality' of most intending immigrants; there were similar responses from administrators in New South Wales, who complained about the colony being used as a dumping ground for paupers (CO 210/443: No. 3658). Experimental colonisation companies were set up to try to improve the quality of person moving to the Australian colonies, but it is clear from, for example, the private correspondence of FitzRoy that these companies were thought to be still not getting it right.

These debates were all conducted with explicit or implicit reference to an assumed-to-be-successful classical practice. The Athenian colonies were said to be bound to Athens by ties of affection precisely because they were like little Athenses, as we have seen. Consequently, the solution to the ills of the Australian colonies was seen in following this example and by introducing the same 'balance' that Britain supposedly enjoyed; the classical influence was important in that it fed attempts to make Australia as like Britain as possible. This influence provided the technical means of governing and aimed at ensuring colonists had an ethical commitment to the empire. In 1858 Edward Lytton, the Secretary of State at the Colonial Office, set up the colonial honours system, which explicitly set out to establish a kind of Australian aristocracy, in spite of Lytton's known dislike for that class. This invention of an honours system served the double function of making the beneficiaries of honours more faithful to Britain and making Australian society more 'balanced'. This was a continuation of the earlier effort by W.C. Wentworth in 1853 to make certain ranks of Legislative Councillors into an hereditary aristocracy (Knox 1992). Other writers in the period dwelt on the lack of a gentry and on the over-representation of men in the Australian colonies (Reports of C.L. and E. Commissioners 24/2/1851, cited in Morrell 1966; The Unknown 1865).

Our argument here, it should by now be clear, is that a variety of solutions to import 'balance' into the Australian colonies were made thinkable by attention to the problems of classical colonisation practices. To return to the city planning examples we mentioned above, the planners of both Melbourne and Adelaide, which were built with streets conforming to a grid pattern, made references to the Greek use of the grid as an appropriate topography for a colony and thereby justified their own choice of the grid. It was seen to have advantages in eliminating dangerous spaces and it made the administration of cities from a distance much more straightforward and rational. So, for example, it was argued that land sales could be more easily supervised from Britain when the plots of land were subjected to the standardising technology of the grid (Davidson 1991). The grid had every requisite quality: it was rational, it was the perfectly 'balanced' architectural form, it allowed for supervision and surveillance, and it was Athenian.

Towards secular ethics

As we have demonstrated at some length, the Greeks were regarded as a model for personal conduct and for administrative excellence, and became briefly very fashionable in Australia. Although the evidence seems to suggest that Hellenism surfaced as an important resource for thinking about the world among elite administrators, the experimental use of Hellenic techniques on the general public should also be considered. Redmond Barry, for example, attempted to extend Hellenism to the public sphere; his vision of Melbourne University, of the State Parliament, and of Melbourne's Public Library was one in which classical styles of architecture must be used and the values of European civilisation upheld. Interestingly, Melbourne Public Library made no attempt to collect any Australiana (Macintyre 1991). Melbourne University, like Sydney, whose motto was, revealingly, *sidere mens eadem mutato*, was from its beginnings an avowedly European institution (Hirst 1988). While Barry was very scathing about his philistine fellow-colonists, as we saw earlier, he still clung to the belief that noble classical buildings could effect an ethical transformation of the citizen body; he believed that the classical style of his buildings could actually provide the city with a much more appropriate and modern secular feel. In the eighteenth century, the ethics of citizenship were the concern of the upper classes; by the nineteenth century, it was thought that far more people in many different social groups were capable of ethical behaviour. This conception of civics drove Barry's various projects in Melbourne.

Barry was a good example of a tendency to rebuild ethical life in a secular direction, a tendency that can be seen in Matthew Arnold's *Culture and Anarchy* (1932). According to Arnold, nineteenth-century life was driven by two ethical tendencies, Hebraism and Hellenism. He characterised Hebraism as 'this paramount sense of the obligation of duty, self-control, and work, this earnestness in going manfully with the best light we have'. Hellenism was 'the intelligence driving at those ideas which are, after all, the basis of right practice, the ardent sense of all the new and changing combinations of them which man's development brings with it, the indomitable impulse to know and adjust them perfectly'. Both aimed at 'man's perfection or salvation', yet they differed in terms of their spontaneity and their moral/ethical flexibility. Arnold regarded Hellenism as the appropriate ethics for a new age of intellectual daring. The British, he thought, had failed to realise that Hebraism should be on the decline and Hellenism in the ascendant (Arnold 1932: 163–8). Of course, we have already met Arnold in the context of the early history of Cultural Studies, and it is perhaps worth reiterating the link here: Arnold's work revolved around a variety of themes that it was almost impossible to unravel in the mid-nineteenth century – culture, order, governance, Hellenism, political economy, the classics, liberalism.

It should be noted that Arnold's was an idiosyncratic reading of Greek culture which stressed the Greeks' ethical rationality, yet many followed Arnold in turning to the Greeks for a way of reconceptualising ethics. No doubt there are many reasons for this move, but perhaps the two most important are the following. First, the Greeks were considered as an example of non-Gospel morality at its sternest. A growing interest in the possibilities of secular democracy, fuelled by liberal philosophy and political practice, no doubt made the Greeks seem pertinent. Second, Hegel's reading of the historical development of Greek philosophy was seen as apposite. Many nineteenth-century thinkers accepted Hegel's view of the passage from *Sittlichkeit* to *Moralität* in Greek civilisation and detected a similar movement in their own age. According to this famous distinction, *Sittlichkeit* constituted the morality residing in the unreflective custom and religion of the ancient community, while *Moralität* was the reflective morality that developed as the individual subjective consciousness looked within itself to discover what objective truth would have moral authority over it. Seen in this light, a renewed interest in the Greeks was perhaps inevitable, and one is tempted to agree with Turner's assertion that by 1850 the effect of works such as

Grote's (1869) *History of Greece* had convinced many that Britain was a mirror image of Athens, that Britain needed to better understand how this ancient naval power had held on to its empire, if the modern naval power that was Britain was to do the same.

Rethinking the governing of Australia: culture as ordering

So far, we have seen how Hellenism provided the intellectual resources for a liberal approach to colonialism and imperial government; there was a close link between a notion of Hellenism as a progressive moral and ethical system and a transformation in the way in which the Australian colonies were governed in the middle of the nineteenth century. We now need to examine more closely how this allowed a set of governing practices to be constructed. As P. Miller (1992) has argued, one of the characteristics of liberal forms of government is less and less its insistence on confrontation, and more and more its concern with the formation of calculative regimes where only the general aims of government are specified. As Miller has it, the logic is in aligning the actions of 'free' individuals with specific objectives by enclosing them within a particular calculative regime. Miller draws on the Nietzsche of the *Genealogy of Morals* when he refers to this as a process of responsibilisation – the formation of calculating individuals who are given responsibility for their own conduct. In theorising a mechanism for this process, Miller draws on Callon and Latour's notion of 'interessement' (cf. Callon 1986); 'interessement' is a kind of fidelity technique, involving the persuasion of those who need to be governed (particularly those who are distant) that they have a series of shared interests with their governors. The formation of a loose and approximate alignment organised around controlling central points is a feature of this process.

In the reconceptualisation of the British Empire as Hellenic rather than Roman in spirit, this move towards a new form of governing as described by Miller can be seen in operation. The Hellenic model was one in which colonies were expected to self-govern, with their faithfulness guaranteed by the *storge,* or bond of affection, they felt towards their mother country. One of the interesting things, for us, about this technique is that, although it was first tried out on colonial administrators, it was pressed into service as a way of convincing the population as a whole to want to be faithful, as is clear from the above discussion of Barry's 'secular ethics'. The Greek noun *storge,* loosely meaning 'love/respect', was frequently used in discussions of the time. It encapsulated the desired relation between Britain and the colonies, and is an emotional state that can be shared by even the humblest colonist (see, for example, Lang 1852: 125).

During the first 50 years of settlement (from 1788) the lands of Australia were administered by officials appointed from Britain, paid from Britain, and considered part of the military. Indeed, their liability was to military rather than civil law (McMartin 1959: 326). The reconceptualisation of the Empire after this period, which was assisted by the impact of Greek thought, can be seen as a new approach to governing at a distance.

First of all, the setting up of a dedicated department to deal with the colonies allowed for the possibility of this new type of governing. The policy of control from the centre would not have been possible without the creation of an effective central department of state devoted to the administration of colonial affairs. This new department was formally in existence in 1801, when Hobart assumed office as Secretary of State for War and the Colonies. It was not, however, until 1812 that effective administration began. Earl Bathurst, who was Secretary of State from 1812 until 1827, and Henry Goulbourn, who was his Deputy from 1812 until 1821, did most of the work involved in constructing an effective administrative department. They built 'a central machinery which could furnish information for the ministry and parliament on colonial affairs' as Helen Taft Manning put it (cited in McMartin 1959: 329; see also Morrell 1966).

During Bathurst's 15 years in charge, many ordered routines and procedures were established in the colonial office. However, while Bathurst, his assistants and successors concentrated on producing an administrative superstructure and on outlining the general aims of the government of the Australian colonies, it is noticeable that government on the spot in Australia was conducted in a rather loose manner. It was quickly realised that most administration needed to be conducted by making use of local talent, and soon colonial civil service regulations made it a condition that the governors keep an eye out for such local talent. For example, this excerpt from the 1843 edition of the regulations makes clear that they aimed at encouraging good recruitment procedures:

> great weight must always be attached to local services and experience. Every Governor will therefore make once in each year a confidential report of the claims of candidates, whether already employed in the public service or not, whom he may consider to possess that qualification. (Great Britain and Ireland – Colonial Office. 1843: 19)

The Governor was responsible for the appointment of magistrates, who were the main means of administering the colonies. These were often local men and their responsibilities tended to be defined by a geographical area rather than attaching to specific functions. Magistrates needed to be very flexible administrators and the flexibility in this role was continued when many of their responsibilities were transferred to the newly reformed police force in 1862. In remote areas the police were often the sole salaried officials, with a large portfolio of jobs. They enforced school attendance, checked the cleanliness of dairies, supervised the storage of gunpowder, kept an eye on orphaned and neglected children boarded out with private families, gave out rations to Aborigines, newly arrived migrants and the infirm, and buried paupers. They were also given responsibility for the collection of statistics and electoral lists. They became collectors of information for policy decisions – for example, they reported on the habits of Chinese immigrants, local larrikins, and the numbers of insane, infirm and destitute (Hirst 1988: 252ff.).

Essentially, then, the good administration of an area depended to a great extent on the talents of local personnel. As James Stephen, in a remark typical of British administrators, put it in a memo in 1841: 'A man of good sense on the spot is far more likely to judge questions correctly than any number of the ablest men at a distance' (CO 201/308, f.12). The use of local talent and the exploitation of existing social circumstances was a device given classical backing in Thucydides, who, incidentally, acted as a kind of guide book for new colonial administrators (Ogilvie 1964). Government was conducted by ensuring an efficient circuit of information from the periphery to the centre, but the actual minutiae of police and magistrate administration was not over-defined. The supremacy of the centre was established by a variety of tactics, including the use of the newly established Colonial Office bureaucracy which acted as a hub for the receipt of information and the issuing of orders (Davidson 1991: ch. 4).

Within Australia the telegraph was used, from the point of view of our concerns, as a means of establishing Sydney and Melbourne as authoritative centres. The first telegraph link was established from Melbourne to Williamstown in 1854; in New South Wales, the first line went up in 1858, and by 1862 the lines reached to the borders of the colony and every substantial town was connected. J.B. Hirst points out how a new town joined the telegraph network long before its roads were made and decades before railway connection (1988: 253). This system enabled rapid communication between police officers, but did not substantially affect the *ad hoc* nature of their practice. The organisation of authoritative centres and responsive peripheries was much more about creating realms of government within which relay points relay administrative power, or act as a means of advising and correcting from a distance. Such forms of government are consonant with the idea of replacing the Roman model of empire with the more subtle model derived from an historically specific reading of Greek practice.

To reiterate Miller's point offered above, the formation of realms of administrative power, loosely linked to each other and to centres, allows a form of control in which direct supervision is unnecessary. The gradual transformation of the Australian public service into a rational bureaucracy (see Beaglehole 1967; Curnow 1975; Loveday 1959; Parker 1989; Roe 1965) installed an additional element, that of expertise, allowing decisions made at the centres to be seen as neutral and objective. It was believed that Australia could be organised according to this centre–periphery model of government and, in addition, that one day the periphery might extend beyond the continent. There was a grander vision of the formation of a distinctively free and moral empire in which the colonies would carry on the British mission. As The Unknown put it (1865: 4):

> Is not this Australia the England of the South? and destined to exercise an influence in the affairs of the world equal, it may be, with that of England itself? With Africa and the English possessions on that continent on the left hand, South America on the right, the Indian Ocean open to the West, and the South Pacific with its numerous islands on the East – these highways of the world – and Australia the central point of the whole, the moral counterpart, and, perhaps, counterpoise of England, what horoscopy is requisite to predict its future?

As we have seen, the cult of Hellenism was one of the ways in which the question of the ethical authority of government could surface; it provided a set of practical means for ensuring certain ethical comportments; and it seems to have 'trickled down' from elite administrators to local magistrates and to the general public. The change of emphasis from the Roman to the Greek was important in allowing a shift from a militaristic and coercive system to one which stressed the utility of moral emulation. The setting up of a model prison on Norfolk Island from 1839 is a good example of this tendency. The prison was intended to be something of a moral reformatory rather than a punishment block and needed to be run by someone of the highest moral calibre. As Lord Normanby put it, the superintendent 'should feel a deep interest in the moral improvement of the convicts' (cited in Kociumbas 1992: 174). Alexander Maconochie eventually took over the superintendent's job and, as his extraordinary guide to prison organisation shows, he took this mission very seriously. As he stated in the preface, 'the object [of the papers in this volume] . . . is . . . to urge the superiority of *moral influence to physical coercion*, where intelligent beings are to be controuled [*sic*] or guided' (Maconochie 1839: Preface, i). This moral influence, which elsewhere he referred to as 'moral surgery', was to be achieved primarily by a system of 'training', which Maconochie distinguished from mere 'instruction':

> The rule or principle, then, is alone inflexible, and must be common to all Superintendents. They must first *punish*, then *train*; – *punish*, if necessary, by *direct physical violence or constraint*, because in this stage it is desirable to subdue the prisoners' minds, and fix them, in painful retrospect, on their past guilt; – but *train*, if possible *exclusively by means of Moral Influence*, – of cheerful animating hope, directed to the future. They must encourage, rather than denounce, or reproach. It is a mistake, much too commonly made, to seek Reform by making Vice painful, instead of making Virtue pleasing and advantageous. This mistake is getting expelled from Schools of Intellect, and it must also quit Schools of Morals. (Maconochie 1839: 100–1)

Maconochie was optimistic enough about this moral retraining of the convicts to 'anticipate a period, (not distant either, were the experiment energetically made), when every species of direct coercive discipline, without exception, might be discontinued at well regulated Training Stations'. This idea

> would have almost every good property as a system of management, and not one bad one as regards the prisoners themselves, for it would be in the highest degree *morally* coercive, yet not physically obligatory at all. Every one would think he enjoyed full freedom of will, – yet every one would be under

the almost absolute controul [*sic*] of impulses, common to all, yet personal to each, and which could not fail, therefore, of generating an *esprit de corps* productive of harmonious effect. (Maconochie 1839: 103–4)

Maconochie's optimism about this moral system and its transformative effects was such that he even advocated the removal of external guards:

I would not myself have a single soldier or professed constable with them – they should themselves enforce the regulations; – nor should I have the slightest fear of hesitation in their being enforced. For why should any hesitate, or rebel? *Habita fides fidem obligat.* (p. 105)

Maconochie – from the perspective of Cultural Studies as the study of ordering – was developing a set of techniques for ensuring fidelity, a system which by privileging self-management and training sought to remove the conflict from prison organisation, enclosing the prisoners instead within a calculative regime where they would be 'responsibilised'.

Concluding remarks

The government of the nineteenth-century Australian colonies required the mastery of a whole series of technical problems. One such technical problem was the morale of administrators and colonists and their faithfulness to the mother-country. One solution lay in the attention to what we have termed fidelity techniques. Fidelity techniques were used to ensure the faithfulness of, at first, the administrators, who were very often not from Britain; and almost immediately thereafter, the population more generally. These fidelity techniques, however, should not be read as some false ideology imposed on an unwilling subject population. The techniques were a way of understanding the business of governing, that is, techniques for ordering governing: while they gave a certain cultural self-confidence to the governors and, ultimately, the population, they must also be seen as productive techniques through which the very notion of citizenship became meaningful.

'Culture' in general was something which could practicably be 'installed' in citizens, and in this way culture and civics could feed into each other. Modes of ethical comportment and techniques of

government should not, in this example, be seen as separate departments of existence, but as coalescing in a mutually productive
relationship. For a very brief period, before an anti-classical reaction
killed Hellenism off, a specific reading of the Greeks provided a way of
establishing a relationship between governor and governed, and thereby
provided an ethics of colonial life. It is important to remember that this
was only one of many possible Hellenisms that could have been taken
up in Australia, and that the accuracy of the nineteenth-century vision
of Athenian colonisation is, in a sense, irrelevant. The contingent,
localised adoption of a certain ethic allowed faithfulness to be recast in
a way consonant with liberal problematisations of authority and with
the problems entailed by government at a distance.

In this chapter we have argued that 'morale', 'confidence' and 'faithfulness', as forms of comportment and self-understanding, need to be
understood as techniques of ordering-as-government which emerged
from a network of heterogeneous elements: in the mid-nineteenth-cen-
tury Australian colonies, these techniques were fashioned out of
Hellenism and liberalism. More specifically, they allowed the formation
of new types of administrator and new types of citizen, locked in place
by the responsibilising regime of the centre–periphery model, and by
their emotional commitment – which had been carefully constructed –
to a far-off power.

Finally, then, in this chapter we have suggested that governing the
colonies required a kind of cultural governance (and remember: culture
is ordering). Australia was governed *through* culture. We can see evidence for two procedures which it is often hard to separate: the
formation of appropriate administrative machines and the formation of
what we term fidelity techniques, or ways of making allegiance to the
centre (in this case, Britain) possible.

It has been necessary, of course, to consider both the government of
others and the government of self. Yet the two are inseparable, because
self-mastery is a precondition for the mastery of others and one aspect
of governing others is teaching them to govern themselves. The main
example we have considered, the civil service, has led us to perhaps privilege the role of bureaucracy in forming techniques of self-government,
although we are of course aware there are other conditions of possibility for the production of the modern self-governing citizen, such as the
Christian pastoral or the humanitarian tradition (as we keep reminding
you, we have more to say about ordering the self later, when we deal

5 Ordering Through the Culture of Law and Regulation

The term 'legal culture' has quite a ring to it, as does 'police culture', 'the culture of the Supreme Court', 'prison culture' or any other term that might be bandied about in attempts to capture some of the more intricate workings of legal and regulatory institutions (in this chapter we use the term 'the culture of law and regulation' to cover all of the above). The 'ring', we suggest, evokes the intricacies of life in courts, law offices, police cars, prisons, etc.

Our aim in this chapter is not to suppress this 'ring' of culture, but to enhance it. It is our view that too many analyses of socio-legal objects rely unthinkingly on the two shibboleths of Cultural Studies we discussed (and criticised) in Chapter 1 – meanings and power. This move, we think, suppresses the 'ring' – it suppresses the search for (and the pleasure in) the intricacies of socio-legal life. Our Cultural Studies as the study of ordering, on the other hand, allows the 'ring' its full resonance.

To let you hear the 'ring' of the culture of law and regulation at its most mellifluous, we mix criticism and exposition. In the first two sections we criticise a few attempts to capture the culture of socio-legal objects, although we try to draw from them the positive possibilities they contain. In the remaining, larger, section we offer an unapologetically positive reading of another sample of socio-legal literature by way of an attempt to show how the culture of law and regulation can be analysed by Cultural Studies as the study of ordering. We begin our critical sections with a section on police culture.

Police culture as complex doing

Richard Ericson and Kevin Haggerty, in *Policing the Risk Society* (1997), provide almost the perfect example of the way the 'ring' of culture can be suddenly and dramatically muted by certain theoretical moves. Their descriptions of certain aspects of police culture-as-ordering could hardly be bettered: wonderful collections of details of the minutiae of police life, in this case focusing on some Canadian police organisations.

Ericson and Haggerty take us to some surprising places in this work. They show us, for instance, that policy manuals are their own form of ordering. In some police organisations, it must be added, they make up a form of ordering that is out of control. In just one manual,

> In well over a thousand pages of rules, one could discover, for example, how to complete different types of forms; create, classify, index, store, deactivate, and destroy records; file things alphabetically; rate the importance of files; prepare monthly returns on the level of 'message traffic' in the communication centre; prevent, investigate and report violations of communication security; pay for and catalogue library books; handle and distribute mail; score data for statistical reporting; ensure the safety of telecommunications technicians; maintain equipment such as radar guns; make and report modifications to communications systems hardware; and communicate using secret codes. (Ericson and Haggerty 1997: 345)

And this is just one small manual. Yes, small: the pool of information contained in manuals for this particular police organisation has grown so large that it is beyond usefulness:

> The police organization with the four-volume manual setting out communication rules [the manuals discussed above] had, in total, twenty-two volumes' worth of manuals of administrative rules. At one point it initiated a program aimed at reducing the total number of administrative-manual pages in circulation. Success was claimed on the basis that a more economical use of page space, a reduction in the number of rules, and, especially the taking of some sets of manuals out of circulation, had lessened the number of pages in circulation from about twenty-eight million to about twenty-one million. However, at the time of our research, the number of pages was beginning to increase again. (Ericson and Haggerty 1997: 348)

We could go on (and on) – the book contains many such wonderful details, that is, many instances of police culture-as-ordering. However, space is limited; we must proceed to our critical argument. Instead of letting their account of police culture ring loud and long, Ericson and Haggerty force our ears to listen to another tune, one we think is far less satisfactory to ears searching for a thorough account of the culture of law and regulation. They do not want us to hear the details of police culture as the end of the story, but merely as signs to a grander tale, a grand tale of 'risk society'. It is a tale that sounds to us like no more than the boring talk of grand power and meaning that we think so problematises most Cultural Studies. They give it a new twist by talking of 'risk', but you should not be fooled. Just look at these quotes:

> Risk society operates within a negative logic that focuses on fear and the social distribution of 'bads' more than on progress and the social distribution of 'goods'. (p. 6)

> Risk society is characterized by the perpetual refinement of rules governing how knowledge is communicated. (p. 9)

> [T]he risk society is also a knowledge society. (p. 8)

These quotes, we contend, could come straight from the Cultural Studies-as-Studies-of-Power-and-Meaning Handbook: gather details, but then drown them in the sea of meaning and power. The 'risk society' which is supposed to be such a revelation looks to us to be the same as the society of meaning and power that was and is continually 'revealed' by Cultural Studies, at least as it is practised by most of its practitioners.

Let us further explore this bizarre ambivalence in Ericson and Haggerty's approach; remember, we contend that they are representative of the majority of work on the culture of law and regulation. In taking existing approaches to task for their limits – 'researchers have been locked into particular frameworks for understanding what the police do'; 'In particular, they have accepted the common view that police officers are primarily agents of criminal law enforcement, and that this agency gives them all of the institutional authority and coercive power necessary to maintain order'; 'Police officers have a similar view of their own work' (p. 11) – Ericson and Haggerty set up their own approach thus:

> Our model provides a new window on policing and the constitutive mechanisms of society. A look through this window reveals many aspects of

policing that have not been brought to light previously. Our new perspective allows us to show the limitations of other theories of policing and to open up new areas for empirical observation and theoretical debate. Risk is a central feature of modernity, and this feature must be interrogated in fine detail and to the fullest possible extent. Risk institutions and their communication systems have become an important basis, and our empirical research on police participation in these institutions and systems substantiates this claim. (1997: 11)

Well, we think it does no such thing. It shows, rather, the perils of grand approaches in Cultural Studies. Ericson and Haggerty's claim that their book 'reveals many aspects of policing that have not been brought to light previously' is spot on. We are deeply indebted to them for this. But the remainder of this assessment of their strengths is ridiculously wide of the mark. Far from the theoretical breakthrough they see, we see only a repetition of the worst excesses of Cultural Studies – wild general claims a long way from the details (details which they so diligently and impressively gather).

When Ericson and Haggerty do what they do best – providing more and more evidence of ordering by police and of police – the results are excellent:

The police sell knowledge in a variety of formats to external institutions. . . . In one police jurisdiction, external institutions that wanted knowledge drawn from police occurrence reports were required to submit a request for information form together with a fifteen-dollar processing fee. . . . The time police officers spent in interviews with insurance adjusters and lawyers was also commodified in some cases. (1997: 342–3)

At this point we should acknowledge a companion on this journey into Ericson and Haggerty's foibles. We are on very similar ground to that pioneered by Pat O'Malley in regard to this book:

[F]or this book, the primary problem created by such grand theorizing is that risk drives out everything else, and is itself moved forward by an objective, inevitable logic. This seems completely incompatible with the Foucaultian ambitions of the authors, and with their own . . . sophisticated observations . . . with respect to the analysis of policework. (1999: 145)

O'Malley surmises that Ericson and Haggerty are driven down the path they take by their overwhelming desire to 'explain the increasing focus on risk technologies and risk information in virtually all major social institutions' (p. 145). He counters: 'For some Foucaultians, at least within the governmentality literature, such explanation is not seen as a necessary step at all, the preferred focus being far more on questions of "how" government works rather than why changes in government come about' (p.145).

While our methodological protocols are built more from Wittgenstein and Pyrrhonism than from Foucault, we can still take this quotation as emblematic of our position here. Indeed, we can rewrite the quotation to describe exactly our position by changing only a few words: 'For us, such explanation is not seen as a necessary step at all, the preferred focus being far more on questions of "how" law and regulation work rather than why changes in law and regulation come about.'

Now we turn our critical attention away from Ericson and Haggerty's wonderful yet frustrating text and towards a couple of other pieces that try to capture the 'ring' of the culture of law and regulation.

The frustration continues

As an example of Cultural Studies operating in US socio-legal studies, consider the following from a piece by Patricia Ewick and Susan Silbey, under the sub-heading 'Consciousness as cultural practice' (1992: 741–2):

> [W]e conceive of consciousness as part of a reciprocal process in which the meanings given by individuals to their world, and law and legal institutions as part of that world, become repeated, patterned and stabilized, and those institutionalized structures become part of the meaning systems employed by individuals. . . . Conceptualized in this way, consciousness is neither fixed, stable, unitary, nor consistent. Instead, we see legal consciousness as something local, contextual, pluralistic, filled with conflict and contradiction.

Sounds promising, does it not? Yet instead of scouring the wonderful details they gather from their impressive 440 interviews about 'ordinary people's legal consciousness', instead of looking for the details of ordering by and about these people, Ewick and Silbey seek help from some of the standard – problematic – resources of Cultural Studies. For instance they invite de Certeau into their parlour. Of course all he does is sidetrack them with his idea that the people have only tactics. Ewick and Silbey thereby throw away their chance to hear the full richness of the ring of culture from their own data set – 'These everyday practices can be thought of as tactical insofar as they are maneuvers within a terrain organised and imposed by a "foreign power"' (1992: 742–3).

In a later piece, Ewick and Silbey (1995) follow a similar trajectory: a potentially fine study of the culture of law and regulation – this time focusing on the various roles of narratives in the operation of law, including, but not limited to, their roles in formal legal proceedings, and featuring, as with their 1992 article, much wonderful detail – is subverted to a particular theoretical agenda. The details of ordering of narratives and by narratives involved in many sites of law and regulation are swamped by the demands of Cultural Studies to bring in power, no matter what. This time it is brought in on the back of an old favourite of Cultural Studies, hegemony.

They put it like this (1995: 211–12):

> Narratives . . . are as likely to bear the imprint of dominant cultural meanings and relations of power as any other social practice. More important, the stories and accounts that are told to and by litigants, clients, lawyers, jurors, and other legal actors are not simply reflective of and determined by those dominant meanings and power relations. They are implicated in the very *production* of those meanings and power relations. . . . It is important to emphasize that narratives do more than simply reflect or express existing ideologies. Through their telling, our stories come to constitute the hegemony that in turn shapes social lives and conduct.

What can we say? Details disappearing, power and hegemony rushing to the front of the stage, shouting loudly and crudely. Of course we could go on and on in this vein, drawing out for praise the elements of legal culture captured in even the most abstract of socio-legal texts yet strongly criticising the way these details are swamped by the imposition of some or other theoretical necessities. But we think we have already said enough for you to catch our drift. Instead, we use the rest of the chapter to draw only positive things from our sources, in a bid to present a picture (more of a sketch) of the culture of law and regulation as seen by Cultural Studies as the study of ordering.

Being positive about the culture of law and regulation

The ring of the culture of law and regulation can best be heard, we reiterate, by listening to (and looking for) the details of ordering. No big sounds (or big pictures) are needed for this type of Cultural Studies (the best type, we suggest). By our approach, and using our method, we can gather details from many investigations. We can use these investigations as the basis for our descriptions of appearances, our descriptions of the appearances of systems of thinking and knowledge, and our descriptions of the uses of appearances. In this way, Cultural Studies as the study of ordering can capture this ring of the culture of law and regulation as most previous formulations of Cultural Studies could not or cannot.

Peter Alldridge, in his evocatively titled 'Attempted murder of the soul' (1993) gives us details about the operation of the law of blackmail. We are handed a bundle of appearances to do with, among other things, attempts to define and deal with blackmail in legislation passed, largely in Britain, between 1827 and 1971, to do with the surprising ways in which threats to behave legally ('I will let everyone know what you've been up to unless . . . ') end up as crimes, and to do with the intricate role of sex (particularly homosexual sex) in blackmail cases. Alldridge also provides us with details of the various ways in which these appearances have been and are systematised (particularly by the law, but also by certain literary devices, especially the crime novel) and the various ways in which they have been and are used (to try to limit blackmail, to advance it, etc.).

Wes Pue provides many details of the culture of law and regulation in his account of the operation of the legal profession in eighteenth- and nineteenth-century Britain and France (Pue 1997). We are presented with details of Paris *avocats* under the *ancien régime* advancing liberal political rights, almost as a trade union, details of their English counterparts of the time (especially barristers) using different tactics (particularly courtroom rhetoric and persuasion, but also pamphletting) to advance similar political ends, details of the intricacies of the Inns of Court, details of the radical Wilkites, and many others. We are also given insight into the ways these appearances have been and are systematised (especially as a history of the political effectiveness of lawyers) and the ways they have been and are used (for instance, as a defence of common law adversarialism).

John Brigham, in his 'The Constitution of the Supreme Court' (1999), produces details about the various aspects of the operation of the US Supreme Court. Here we are invited to deal with appearances of architecture, dress, interior design, and ritualistic behaviours, among others. Brigham also supplies details about some of the ways in which these appearances have been and are systematised (not just into binding protocols, but also into journalistic tropes) and some of the ways in which they have been and are used (particularly in fostering and/or resisting 'the cult of the court' and even 'the cult of the judge').

It should already be clear that most socio-legal pieces can be mined for 'ringing' evidence of the culture of law and regulation. It is a veritable gold rush – the nuggets are lying about on the ground of socio-legal publishing. So why do not more people pick them up? We think many scholars simply do not see them because the theoretical yokes they pull on (perhaps as penance?) do not allow a view of the ground. Our method is simple – in treating appearances seriously, this method not only allows a view of the ground, indeed, it pretty much forces the eyes down (and the mind with it). Yes, we are celebrating a certain porcine quality – roll in the mud of the socio-legal and you might well enjoy the richness of the soil. Any era, any society – the details of the culture of law and regulation can be gathered from most places and times you care to look.

If you have become worried that we are putting too much stress on details, then maybe you are thinking of 'details' in the wrong way. We accept that the devil is in the detail, so if you think 'detail' is too small a space to fit both the devil and the culture of law and regulation, chances are you are thinking of 'detail' as a phone booth in a field of theory. Forget the theory and the details become the field – plenty of room for everyone. Remember, our method is not out to 'explain' culture or to 'reveal' its 'causes'. No, we are demonstrating, we hope, that to highlight the myriad appearances of myriad cultures, the ways they are systematised and the ways they are used, is to perform high-quality intellectual work, full stop.

Less talk, more culture please.

Andrew Borkowski (1994) is not one to back away from the richness of socio-legal soil. He goes to the garden of Roman socio-legal life and finds wonderful details seemingly wherever he turns. We shall go with him to just one, somewhat unusual, spot in the garden (unusual for the twenty-first-century scholar) – the ownership and management of slaves.

Slavery, Borkowski tells us (the details in this example are taken entirely from his 1994 textbook, ch. 4), was central to Roman life. The Romans defined slavery in terms of loss of freedom and tried to treat slaves, legally, as 'things', although they were never able to do this completely. Slaves were always owned, but they could be owned by the state as well as by individuals. The living conditions of Roman slaves varied by time and place – they were worst in rural areas and at times of oversupply (when many captured peoples were made slaves). Legally, one could become a slave in four ways: (i) by birth (being born to a slave mother, no matter what the status of the father); (ii) by punishment (various crimes attracted this punishment, including theft, evasion of taxes and census, ingratitude on the part of freed slaves, and fraud involving attempts to sell free people into slavery); (iii) by being sold into slavery at birth (parents could buy their children back later if their circumstances improved); (iv) by capture (the source of the most slaves, especially in the late Republic when the Roman armies under Caesar overran Gaul).

Various legal rules were developed to deal with the contingencies of slavery. For instance, the legal position of slaves became a complex matter – while masters were technically free to do as they pleased with slaves, they could suffer disgrace if they treated them brutally. (Hadrian introduced measures to prevent masters from castrating slaves and from putting them to death without the permission of a magistrate; by Justinian's time, under the influence of Christianity, masters were restricted to 'reasonable chastisement'.)

Slaves were held responsible for crimes they personally committed, though they could not be called as witnesses against their masters and they could not be held liable for delicts (or civil wrongs). In such cases the master was held responsible and entered the procedure of the noxal surrender of slaves (whereby the slave responsible for the delict had to be surrendered, or could be so surrendered, to the person wronged by the delict). Slaves technically could not own property, but various legal means were found whereby they could enjoy considerable amounts of property. This was also true for the making of contracts and the forming of personal relationships. In the latter case, while marriage between slaves was not permitted (or between slaves and citizens), various rules had to be formulated for the children produced by the sexual unions of such groupings.

A final important point for our attention concerns the freeing of slaves. By far the most important means was manumission, or the freeing of slaves by the master. Manumission could be performed formally, in front of a senior magistrate, but it could also be done by the slave being enrolled on the census with the master's permission. As well, it could be done by will (though testators could impose conditions on this, which led to many regulations), it could be done by the Church (in Christian times), and it could be done informally – when a master had acted for a reasonable time as if his slave were freed, though he had not formally taken the steps to free him. The great Roman legal reformers, Augustus and Justinian, each reformed the manumission laws considerably (Augustus between 2 BC and AD 19; Justinian between AD 527 and 534).

Not a long way from this theme, Peters (1985) provides fruit for our sideboard in his discussion of some of the conditions which allowed the legal use of torture to flourish in ancient Greece and Rome. The notion of status was crucial. Those with status, especially citizens, but even some foreigners (especially metics – a category of foreigners important largely for their role in commerce), were considered to be truthful as a matter of honour. It was very rare for them to be tortured. Torture evolved as a device for establishing the truth of testimony of those without honour, especially slaves.

The system of law which had emerged from feud and blood feud was still based on citizen accusation. The big new development was a consistent system of judgements built up, often with the aid of recording, and applied by a non-disputant (in the first instance another citizen, but eventually specialists and sometimes panels). In line with this came a procedure for producing reliable evidence – a consistent body of knowledge gained by various means to establish truth in the eyes of the law. Without this, torture, as a public legal device, might not have developed (although of course it was already well developed as random violence and as a means of political intimidation). It seems that the logic of the ancients was something like this: slaves cannot know truth as they have no honour, and they are not persons in any legal or moral sense; for their testimony to count in such an honourable and moral process as law, jurists must be certain they are telling the truth; torture is the best way of being certain.

Torture was thus used on slaves as a matter of procedure, though subject to certain rules (not in any case against their own master, only for certain charges, in line with a code of torture, etc.). Torture was occasionally used against citizens, but only in the case of offences which were seen to threaten the stability of the city or Empire, such as treason. In this way, torture was distinct from capital punishment – its ends were very different, even though the methods may have been similar and even though the outcome of torture was often death.

The Romans under the Republic did not use legal torture as much as had the Greeks. The legal system of republican Rome sought recourse to it only under very strict conditions and only ever against non-citizens, especially slaves. And where only a few Greek jurists expressed reservations about the use of torture, many republican Roman jurists wrote on its limitations and problems. However, the shift to imperial Rome marked a return to Greek levels of the use of legal torture. Sometimes this was simply a matter of the whims of particular emperors (Caligula is an infamous example). More important, however, was the shift in conditions that allowed Rome's carefully built system of law an ever-wider reach, as emperors, particularly in times of war, perceived more and more enemies. Increasingly, even groups of citizens were subjected to judicial torture, a development which was spurred on by the creation, albeit over several centuries, of two categories of citizen, *honestiores* and *humiliores*. The latter group were eventually seen to be as torturable as slaves and even the former group came to be more and more subject to torture, as they were increasingly viewed as potential rivals to the emperor.

Brown et al. (1990: ch. 2) furnish us with many details about the culture of crime by juxtaposing a borrowing from Malinowski's (1926) account of the Trobriand Islands in the early part of the twentieth century to a borrowing from Hay's (1975) account of what counted as crime in tenth- to twelfth-century England. They employ Malinowski's story of a ritual suicide and its aftermath – a youth of about 16 dressed himself in his full ceremonial gear, climbed a coconut tree, shouted accusations, using insults regarded as deeply injurious, against a former lover who had recently accused him in public of having broken the rules of exogamy with his maternal cousin, then jumped to his death; at his funeral a quarrel broke out in which his accuser was deliberately wounded. Brown et al. then discuss the ways in which such a 'killing' and wounding are foreign to our modern Western criminal law and follow this by contrasting Malinowski's story with some details from Hay et al. Among this latter group of details are: in Anglo Saxon England there were 'no courts, codes and constables which we normally associate with the criminal law'; redress for aggrieved individuals was left in their hands or those of their kin – 'If one person injured another, compensation rather than punishment was the principal concern' (loss of one eye was worth so much, loss of two so much, loss of a leg so much, etc.; higher rates applied to people of higher rank, etc.); this system gave way to a system whereby people committed themselves to a powerful protector for protection against invaders, particularly the invading Vikings; after the Norman Conquest of 1066 and the unification it brought, a new set of arrangements came into play as feudalism developed the idea that an injury to a person was also an injury to that person's lord.

Brown et al. thereby provide quite a boost to our point that the culture of law and regulation can only be located in the details. Period-hopping and society-hopping investigations are wonderful repositories of such details, but they are not 'lessons' in the way a theory of legal culture drawn from standard Cultural Studies would have it. They tell us what they tell us. The only general point we get from them is that the culture of law and regulation is rich and diverse; they have no deep meaning; they reveal nothing about other instances of the culture of law and regulation. They are instances of appearances of law and regulation and of the different ways these appearances are systematised and used.

Continuing with our period-hopping, we turn now to van Caenegem and his (1991) comparison between the operation of criminal law in England and Flanders in the twelfth century. Both countries were ruled by princes concerned with imposing order – Henry II and Philip of Alsace, both famed as legal innovators and law-givers. Van Caenegem's particular concern is with two sets of measures: the Assizes of Clarendon and Northampton of 1166 and 1176 and the Great Borough Charter for Flemish towns (1165–77). Henry's Assizes created a centralised system for the prosecution of serious crimes, including robbery, murder, theft and receiving (forgery and arson were added later). The aim was to catch those escaping the net of private prosecutions. Twelve men of the Hundred (a group of rulers), and four men of every township, were sworn under oath of royal authority to identify those suspected of these crimes. The accused were then sent to the ordeal of water and if they failed they were punished by the loss of a foot (later a right hand) and banishment. Those who succeeded at the ordeal but who were seen by the testimony of many men to be of bad repute were also sent into exile. It was made clear that this was a royal exercise and was not the province of any lord. No one was exempted from participating in the sworn indictments, no one could refuse entry to the king's sheriffs. Royal authority thus imposed itself as a supplement to private forms of accusation.

In Flanders, Philip created a system of uniform laws based upon a network of urban courts in which aldermen, appointed by Philip, gave judgements in his name. Punishment was usually by death or ruinous fine for serious crimes (forgery and theft, later joined by rape and murder). Proof was by inquest by the aldermen rather than by ordeal (a remarkably rational move for this time). Prosecutions were still mainly private but sometimes one of Philip's officials launched prosecutions. Fines were paid to Philip's fisc and there were legislative checks on the power of the urban courts, both measures which increased centralised authority.

The culture of law and regulation is indeed fascinating. And it is complex. In this example, the fact that justice administration was a major source of revenue complicates the culture of law and regulation by implicating the ordering of the fisc in the ordering of criminal populations. Another complication, in the Flanders instance, was the tendency of some towns to regard their relations with other towns ahead of the idea of punishing crime for social governance reasons. In these towns emphasis was placed upon reconciliation and compensation ahead of punishment, creating a very different culture of law and regulation.

Van Caenegem is keen that we also note the differences between the English and Flemish reforms (in our terms, cultural differences). Perhaps the most obvious is that Henry's reforms could cover the whole of England where Philip's reforms were restricted to certain (admittedly important) towns. Other key differences include the different crimes selected for punishment (for example, in Flanders they left out arson; a strange omission in towns mainly built of wood) and in the different punishments used. In Flanders there was something of a tradition of counts carrying out the punishments themselves (for example, Count Baldwin VII – Baldwin the Axe – travelled with his own axe to execute criminals, if he did not choose to boil them alive; other bizarre Flemish punishments included beheading with a plank, for some rape cases), while the English situation was much more likely to include particular mutilations but not death. (Historians debate why the death penalty was so rarely used by the royal English at this time – possibly because the central authorities thought mutilations more of a deterrent or, more likely, because they were wary, in imposing their new centralising moves, of losing authority with the use of too many death penalties.)

Hopping to the twentieth century, our method deals just as simply with the culture of the Australian legal profession. In this example we treat some details from Pat O'Malley (1983: 73–91) as an account of appearances and the way they are systematised and used, a way to hear this particular ring of the culture of law and regulation.

O'Malley tells us that Australian lawyers are very tightly organised, something which has been achieved despite the fact that any Australian may represent him or herself legally, whereas, for instance, he or she cannot legally do electrical work on a house. This is to say that the gate-keeping mechanisms of the Australian legal profession – the various state associations, overseen by the different Supreme Courts – are very strong. They even have the power to determine university curricula, or at least to influence it. More than this, the socialisation of young lawyers into a particular ethic and lifestyle is also strong.

Various divisions over the years since European settlement, especially that between barristers and solicitors, have served to cement to the overall strength of the legal profession, rather than to weaken it – the social homogeneity of the legal profession is quite marked. O'Malley says the notion of 'the rule of law' plays a crucial role in this unity, convincing lawyers and others of the necessity of an autonomous legal profession. This is not to say that within the Australian legal profession there are no internal divisions – of course there are specialisms, almost sub-professions. While these have led to some internal status disputes (criminal lawyers versus commercial; public lawyers, especially 'community' lawyers versus private), as with the division between barristers and solicitors, the overall effect has been to strengthen rather than weaken the overall autonomy of the legal profession as a whole.

Staying in the twentieth century but returning to the culture of police, Hogg (1987: 121–37) considers some aspects of the control of criminal investigations, specifically in the Australian jurisdiction of New South Wales. He discusses the difficulties of using crime 'clear up rates' as a measure of investigative performance (especially the tendency to force police towards trivial, easy-to-resolve cases and towards a mentality of 'thief taking' primarily using 'inside information'), but also notes their survival as an administrative tool. Concentrating on internal rules and 'culture' rather some general notion of 'the law', Hogg discusses the cultivation of informers as a long tradition in Australian policing. He provides wonderful details of the ways in which police officers are officially encouraged (albeit with caveats) to keep in close friendly social contact with known criminals and their families.

On similar ground, Hogan (1988: 80–9), furnishes excellent details about police use of firearms in New South Wales, especially in regard to the process of arming and training, the 'culture' of gun use and the difficulty of internally and externally policing this use of firearms. In a separate piece from that drawn on above, Hogg (1988: 61–77) provides details about police use of motor vehicles in New South Wales, especially in regard to training, the 'culture' of car use, the difficulty of internally and externally policing this use and possible alternatives to car use.

Hopping back in time again, Christina Larner (1981: ch. 9) provides a feast of details about the process of prosecuting witches in seventeenth century Scottish courts. The character or repute of accused witches, she tells us, was very important in the legal process of the time (the notion of *mala fama* being crucial for a prosecution). Some witches were caught up in a mass hunt mentality, others were accused after long histories of battles with neighbours. The Kirk (Church) was the first court to hear the charges and the Kirk sessions had to decide whether to proceed with each case by submitting it to the Privy Council. They could also banish the accused (robbing them of their livelihoods) or impose minor penalties.

Larner says that the Kirk sessions knew the sort of evidence that would allow cases to proceed. *Mala fama* was so important because it implied the 'pact with the devil' (renunciation of baptism, sex with the Devil, becoming the Devil's servant) that was at the heart of proving a person was a witch. The 'proof' involved was, more often than not, an extracted confession. Methods for extracting confessions included sleep deprivation, threats of other torture and direct torture. Scotland was closer to Roman law than to English common law in its use of torture to extract confessions or implicate others, though there was some disquiet about its use. Scotland did not have the rack, but it did have cashielaws (leg crushers, known as 'the boots'), pinniewinks (thumbscrews), burning with hot irons, and tearing out nails, not to mention the threat of torturing relatives of the accused (this last was thought, even in Scotland at this time – quite used to torture – to be barbaric).

As well as torture there were the ordeals. These were not about confession but about evidence, Scotland at this time was still employing methods whereby evidence involved looking for signs from God. 'Swimming the witch' (throwing her bound into a pool to see if she floated – the Devil's help) was a rarely used ordeal in Scotland at the time. Laying hands on a corpse to check for special marks was more common, as was testing the reaction of horses to the accused, but witch pricking was by far the most common form of ordeal. 'Witch pricking' was a process whereby an 'expert' pricked parts of the body of the accused to determine whether the Devil had left his mark, in which case, it was thought, the skin would be insensitive to the prick. This procedure was eventually seen to be unreliable (even fraudulent), but it survived as a legal procedure for quite some time, Larner argues, because it served as a link between popular and official belief. It was used as a means of tutoring the wider population of the dangers of association with the Devil.

The Privy Council stage of witch prosecutions was usually handled locally – the Council had the power to grant local commissions. This localisation had the effect, according to Larner, of including local elites (lords, large landholders) in such an important governmental initiative. The local level included both trial and executions. The executioner was usually the local locksmith and he was given a few days to prepare the fuel for burning the witch. Each execution was a big local event, perhaps preceded by days of fasting and prayer. Thousands often attended the event. Usually the witch was garrotted before being burnt, though occasionally witches were burned alive (the accompanying torment and blaspheming by the victims were the source of lessons for the spectators, according to the Church).

Despite the nature of the prosecution procedure, which sometimes dragged on for months or years for lack of evidence, the suspect being imprisoned the whole time, it was far from certain. It was, Larner argues, inefficient and somewhat random. As well as the fairly common occurrences of escape before trial and suicide (presenting difficulties in that the proper disposal of the body of a charged but unconvicted witch was a matter of debate; some bodies were dragged out and punished anyway), sometimes the outcome was banishment, admonition or even acquittal. A common successful defence was a slander charge against the accuser. Another relatively successful route was appeal by lawyer against conviction (only open to those who could afford it). The success rate for avoiding convictions went up dramatically after the first wave of witch hunts and was up to about 50 per cent by 1700.

Conclusion: enjoying limited realism and nominalism

There you have it: legal culture, prison culture, police culture, the culture of the legal profession and other such 'cultures' need not be about power and are not necessarily made up of meanings. Sticking to appearances (and the appearances of their systematisations and uses) presented to us by a variety of published sources, we have given you an account of different instances of the culture of law and regulation that pushes power and meaning off the stage.

It will not have escaped your attention, we trust, that in doing what we have done, we have embraced nominalism, at least to some degree. Nominalism need not be a handicap. Indeed, it is only a handicap if your aim is to produce general accounts that carry 'messages' for others. If your aim is to stick to careful accounts of particular instances of some objects – in this case the different cultures we are calling the culture of law and regulation – nominalism is a boon. It is all too easy to be seduced by the siren song of the general claim.

Please note carefully: the account offered above is not an indication of the grand picture of legal culture we want to impose on you as an alternative to that posed by the various contenders in the battle for Cultural Studies. It is far less ambitious. It is a disparate collection of accounts of particular instances of certain sets of details we call instances of the culture of law and regulation. No more, no less. The stress is on the instances. We employ the term 'the culture of law and regulation' as a convenient shorthand – in some sense because we are forced to do so by that which has gone before us: addressing debates about culture necessitates some use of the terms of that debate (in other words, we have to use some term or other that has some currency).

We do not, for a minute, suggest there is some big object – CULTURE – that we must try to put into a bag more quickly and efficiently than others have done. But this does not mean we are rejecting realism altogether. Like Tom Osborne (1998), we suggest we are employing a very limited realism. For us, there really are appearances (and the appearances of their systematisations and uses) and these are what we try to describe to you. It is a nominalist-limited realism in that we never suggest these appearances come together to form larger objects. The culture of law and regulation, like other cultures, never grows beyond its appearances.

6 Ordering Through the Culture of Everyday Life

Remember our cutlery freaks? Remember our fridge? They of the ordering brigade. Oh yes, we are sure you remember them and their ilk, and we are confident they intrigue you, as they intrigue us. We suspect you know there is at least a little bit of them in you, in all of us. We want to take you closer to them in this chapter (well, not too close) and explore the culture of everyday ordering. If you want a summary statement of what is involved in such an exploration, you will not find better than this one by Georges Perec:

> What we need to question is bricks, concrete, glass, our table manners, our utensils, our tools, the way we spend our time, our rhythms. To question that which seems to have ceased forever to astonish us. We live, true, we breathe, true; we walk, we open doors, we go down staircases, we sit at a table in order to eat, we lie down on a bed in order to sleep. How? Where? When? Why?
>
> Describe your street. Describe another street. Compare.
>
> Make an inventory of your pockets, of your bag. Ask yourself about the provenance, the use, what will become of each of the objects you take out.
>
> Question your tea spoons.
>
> What is there under your wallpaper? (Perec 1997: 206–7)

What, indeed?

We indicated in an earlier chapter that the Sacks/Silverman team gives us heart in studying the intricacies of everyday ordering. Sacks went as far as to invent particular methods to try to track just a few aspects of everyday ordering through conversation. We shall not be following him all the way on this remarkably fine-tuned journey. It just is not within the scope of this book: when we tell you that Sacks devised a way of transcribing every utterance, pause, breath and gesture of each fraction of a second of everyday conversations, you will see not only the source of our admiration for him and those who follow him closely, but also that ours is a much more introductory project, designed to introduce the broader idea of ordering to Cultural Studies. Nonetheless, we can and do make hay from a further sunny meeting with the Sacks/Silverman duo.

We use some of what they have to say about everyday conversations as the basis for our first main section. Three other main sections follow: one based on some of Bill Bryson's detailed and decidedly iconoclastic descriptions of everyday life in America over several centuries – *Made in America* (1994); one based on another text we have already introduced – Weber's *The Protestant Ethic and the Spirit of Capitalism* (1989); and one based on the remarkable glimpse of everyday life in the ancient world captured by Paul Veyne in his contributions to the volume he edited for the *History of Private Life* project (Volume 1: *From Pagan Rome to Byzantium* [1992]).

Conversing the everyday, ordering the everyday

Silverman notes, in introductory voice:

> An old Lancashire saying is that 'There's nowt so queer as folk.' The assumption that ordinary people often behave in crazy and unintelligible ways provides endless material for the tabloid media. But is such behaviour always crazy? and is it unintelligible? . . . Sacks shows us that some apparently bizarre behaviour is not crazy or random but skilful and often routinized. (Silverman 1998: 1–2)

There is method in the madness that is ordering.

Silverman considers Sacks's investigation of how statements about the possibility of committing suicide can be treated as jokes.

> Our laughter means that we have honoured one kind of social duty: someone has told a joke and we have provided an appreciation of it. Moreover, our laughter (the appreciation) has the neat consequence of bringing the activity to an end (that is, the telling of a joke is completed by the laughter) and we are now out of this topic. So a workable solution to this kind of moral dilemma is to turn a potentially challenging, non-routine 'cry for help' into one of the many ceremonial forms (like jokes or greetings) that are a routine part of the everyday world that we inhabit. (Silverman 1998: 2)

Silverman also reports on Sacks's handling of less dramatic examples. Sacks gives us insight into the routine occurrence of ritual attempts at 'getting to know you'. He shows how questions to someone we might be keen to get to know are the most likely ice-breakers because it is conventionally very difficult to refuse to answer. Moreover, for the questioner, even a token response provides a legitimate opportunity for a follow-up question:

A: When does the plane arrive?

B: 7:15.

A: Are you going to San Francisco also? (Sacks, quoted in Silverman 1998: 4)

Sacks allows us to see the way this simple device becomes slightly more complex in a crowd, for instance involving 'territorial' manoeuvres, as when someone offers to buy drinks for everyone at a table and then tries to position both the drinks and him/herself such that he/she is next to the person of desire. As Silverman notes, 'These various devices underline Sacks's point that the achievement of a two-party conversation is a skilful, collaborative accomplishment' (pp. 4–5).

Everyday ordering is clearly a complex business. The culture of the everyday is, as with the culture of law and regulation, or any other set of cultures we refer to in the singular for ease of expression, a treasure-trove of details of ordering. For us, carefully describing the appearances of these details (and the appearances of their systematisations and their uses) is the best way to study this culture of the everyday. Raymond Williams's famous claim, mentioned earlier, that culture is ordinary seems to have been the starting-gun for a race to find meaning and power in all aspects of daily living. We're now crying 'Stop!' Culture is indeed ordinary, but as we said in Chapter 1, it is ordinary in being ordering. In this chapter, in concentrating on discussions of everyday examples, we are concentrating on that most ordinary of beasts, everyday culture as ordering.

Silverman says, 'Sacks is showing us . . . that, in practice, we construct our talk by reference to how it will be heard. By saying what we do, positioned in a certain place, we thus make available to our hearer(s) a particular *reading*' (p. 6). In other words, we order our selves, very finely (an idea that becomes central to this chapter in its later sections). Consider the ordering of our selves necessary to observe certain codes of etiquette. Silverman discusses Sacks's use of guides to etiquette in establishing the necessity of lying.

From these it becomes clear that the person who answers 'truthfully' to a ceremonial question ['How are you?'; 'How do you do?'] has all the makings of a bore. By contrast, by sometimes 'lying' when asked such a question, we show proper concern for what we and others should properly do. . . . On the one hand, we are never supposed to lie. On the other, we would place people in an unwelcome position if we failed to show concern with 'the different consequences of . . . alternative answers'. . . . [O]f course, the maxim 'everyone has to lie' will be heard as appropriate only to *certain* occasions. (Silverman 1998: 7)

Much hinges, it seems, on the position of our conversational utterances, especially on our taking our turn to speak (or perhaps speaking out of turn). Consider the following example of a conversation between two people about to order a meal:

A: I'm going to have X.

B: Well I just had that so I'll have Y.

or:

A: I'm going to have X.

B: I don't like that. (Silverman 1998: 8)

Silverman, quoting Sacks, concludes (p. 9):

In such cases 'you deal with their choice as if they were proposing it for you.' Why? The answer lies in the fact that, although A is addressing a waiter, you hear A as saying something of possible relevance to you. After all, it is likely to be your turn next. . . . So choices by two people or more from a restaurant menu, like greeting exchanges or proverb assertions, are cooperatively accomplished.

The culture of the everyday even provides its own techniques for determining what counts as evidence. As the Silverman/Sacks team puts it (p. 13):

[P]eople are only entitled to have experiences in regard to events that they have observed and/or which affect them directly. . . . In this way, Sacks notes, we turn events into experiences or 'something for us.' However, this shows that telling someone our experiences is not just emptying out the contents of our head but organizing a tale told to a proper recipient by an authorized teller. In this sense, experiences are 'carefully regulated sorts of things'.

In other words, the protocols of everyday conversations include devices for establishing what is to count as true. That these devices are different from those employed in laboratories and different again from those employed in law courts is grist for the mill of our argument that the only way to come to grips with different cultures is to pay attention to their details, their specificities.

It almost goes without saying that the boundary between 'the everyday' and other spheres of existence that we commonly refer to by particular names is always a shifting and blurred one. For example, take the sphere of 'the political' and instances of racism. It is far from clear where 'the everyday' stops and 'the political' starts, to the point where we might profitably think of 'everyday politics'. Silverman/ Sacks give us a lead in describing some of the intricacies of this type of politics:

> [Consider] the methods used by racists to link particular 'evils' to the work of people with certain identities (such as Catholics, Jews, blacks). We identify people by choosing one of many categories that could be used to describe them. It then follows that . . . 'any person who is a case of a category is seen as a member of a category, and what's known about that category is known about them, and the fate of each is bound up in the fate of the other'. (Silverman 1998: 17)

Of course an everyday politics of racism should not be singled out as somehow more important than other aspects of everyday ordering. As Silverman puts it, while 'part of this ordering and constructing our affairs does create activities like racism . . . it also allows us to treat each other as [for example] professional and clients', among many, many other things. Silverman/Sacks raise the possibility that everyday ordering can produce a politics of a much more subtle kind than that found in racism. For example, it may be a politics concerned with the control of terminology: 'Freud faced the difficulty that everybody considers themselves an expert in psychology. Perhaps this is why Freud sought to invent new terms and attempted to enforce how they were used' (pp. 18–19).

We said we would not take you too far with Sacks/Silverman, pulling up short of an examination of the two strict methodological devices Sacks formulated. But this does not mean we cannot usefully extract a few more points about the intricacies of ordering through everyday conversation from Silverman's exposition of one of these devices – Conversation Analysis. We have already glimpsed that part of Conversation Analysis which deals with the fact that participants in conversations take turns to speak (or sometimes take others' turns). In expanding this, Silverman takes us into other aspects of this methodological device, including those dealing with procedures for changing speakers, adjacency pairs, the rules for appropriateness of placing contributions to conversations, and rules of 'chaining' (pp. 104–9). In explaining the notion of adjacency pairs, Silverman says it refers to the phenomenon of consecutive conversational utterances that have the effect of constraining the second speaker – for example greeting necessitates response, question necessitates answer, and so on. He draws on Sacks in pointing to the two basic features the conversation analyst should look for: 'First, the two parts are "relatively ordered" and what should be done is "specified by the pair organization." Second, if the indicated second is not done it will be "seen to be absent" and a repeat of the first will be offered' (p. 105).

Silverman (pp. 107–8) explains the notion of 'chaining' as an extension of that of adjacency pairs – whereby a longer sequence of, for instance, questions and answers establishes a 'chain' such that speakers become enmeshed in the sequence.

> Sacks illustrates this 'chaining rule' through a classic Yiddish joke. A young man (A) finds himself on a train sitting next to an older man (B). This conversation then ensues:
>
> 'A: Can you tell me the time?
>
> B: No.
>
> A: What do you mean no?
>
> B: If I tell you the time we will have to get into a conversation. You'll ask me where I'm going. It will turn out we're going to the same place. I'll have to ask you for dinner. I have a young marriageable daughter, and I don't want my daughter to marry someone who doesn't wear a watch.'
>
> B's wariness about answering a question shows the power of the 'chaining rule'. . . . (Silverman 1998: 108)

This leads Silverman to a discussion of Sacks's awareness of the complexity of ordering through conversation. In effect, Silverman/Sacks give an illustration of our point that ordering is never complete:

> Sacks is very aware of the dangers of a purely mechanistic reading of anything he calls a rule. This leads to three notes of caution. First, obviously, because questioners can ask a further question, this does not mean that they will actually do so. Second . . . adjacency need not mean that the answer will be produced in the very next turn. Finally, relatedly, when questions

produce further questions, this can sometimes turn the chaining rule around. So, as in the case of 'You know what Mommy?', children set up a situation where they revert to an answering role as a result of the predictable . . . response of 'What?' (Silverman 1998: 108).

And not only does ordering have limits, the study of ordering (itself, of course, an exercise in ordering) has limits – as we keep saying, there is no possibility of a general theory of ordering. Ordering, whether through conversation, or some other everyday means, or any means for that matter, must be studied through its details. Ordering is not a substitute for a general theoretical category like power.

We can leave ordering through conversation there and head to some other aspects of everyday culture, this time focusing particularly on aspects of American everyday ordering, as seen through the eyes of Bill Bryson. But just before we do, let us hear again from Georges Perec, by way of reinforcing the idea that everyday ordering has limits, even if we sometimes try to pretend otherwise:

> Like the librarians of Babel in Borges's story, who are always looking for the book that will provide them with the key to all the others, we oscillate between the illusion of perfection and the vertigo of the unattainable. In the name of completeness, we would like to believe that a unique order exists that would enable us to accede to knowledge all in one go. (Perec 1997: 151)

How true. Studying culture as ordering will help us keep this troubling thought at bay.

America the ordered

Bryson's text is hardly your standard Cultural Studies fare and is certainly not a book directly about ordering. But, as is our habit, we find many wonderful details of ordering by picking through material kindly provided for us by other scholars. And Bryson is certainly a scholar – while *Made in America* (1994) may be marketed as a popular book by a very popular author, this should not in any way blind academic readers to its careful approach to the study of processes of ordering. The book is subtitled *An Informal History of the English Language in the*

United States, but we contend it is only this in passing. A more accurate subtitle would be 'Ordering Everyday American Life Since European Settlement'. Sounds ambitious, does it not, but this is what we think Bryson has, perhaps inadvertently, pulled off. Of course you will get only a flavour of his achievement from us – we borrow no more than a handful of insights from the second half of the book in a bid further to secure our Cultural Studies as the study of ordering – and we shall leave it to you to go right to the source and ask the horse.

We begin with one of the most everyday of American ordering devices – the shopping mall.

> The man responsible for the layout and ambience of the modern shopping center was not an American but a Viennese named Victor Gruen, who fled the Austrian Anschluss in 1938. . . . Within twelve years he had become one of the country's leading urban planners. . . . Gruen's intention was not to create a new and more efficient way of shopping but to recreate in America something of the unrushed cafe-society atmosphere of European city centers. . . . Gruen was convinced that he was designing a system that would slow suburban sprawl and tame the automobile. How wrong he was. (Bryson 1994: 215)

After differentiating the shopping mall from the older idea of the arcade and after discussing the etymology of the word 'mall', Bryson details Gruen's wishful thinking – shopping 'towns' in which people stroll ('get out of their cars and onto their feet') and enjoy a sense of community amid fountains and sculptures, encouraged to sit and relax. In 1956 Gruen's vision 'was given tangible shape with the construction of the Southdale Center in the Minneapolis suburb of Medina',

> the biggest shopping center in the world, and the commercial wonder of its age. Reporters came from almost every large newspaper and magazine to marvel at its ten acres of enclosed shopping area, seventy-two stores, and forty-five acres of parking space for 5,200 cars. It became the model from which all other malls in America were cloned. (Bryson 1994: 216)

We hardly need add that this everyday institution spread rapidly through many other countries.

Bryson even allows us a glimpse of the shopping mall 'science' that sprang to life, and some of its consequences:

> At their conferences, mall planners bandied about concepts like *Reilly's Law of Retail Gravitation* (essentially, the mix of stores necessary to keep people moving) and *optimal positional isochrones* (another way of saying

that the best location for a shopping center is near a highway interchange).
No one any longer thought about the idea of encouraging people to linger
or socialize. Benches were built without backs so that people *wouldn't*
linger on them, and food court tables given just enough crampedness to
induce a sense of discomfort after about ten minutes. Victor Gruen's vision
of people sitting with cappucinos, reading newspapers on gripper rods provided by a thoughtful management, or playing chess beside whispering
fountains never materialized. (Bryson 1994: 216)

Even if we allow for a little poetic licence here on Bryson's part, it is
surely safe to say that shopping malls have not turned out anything like
Gruen's dream as a means of achieving a civilised ordering of everyday
life. But, it is equally safe to say, the shopping mall certainly became a
powerful everyday force for ordering. Older, slower ways of shopping
and socialising, based on British and European developments like 'high
street' shopping, 'cafe society', and centralised inner-city commercial
life (what Americans call 'downtown') were quickly rolled back as features of life for many, perhaps the majority of, citizens of 'advanced'
Western nations. Bryson's focus may be the USA, but we suggest the
following details he provides about the growth of 'mall life' are at least
indicative of trends in Britain, Australasia, Canada and much of
Europe and Asia:

> By the early 1980s, the United States had twenty thousand large shopping
> centers, which between them accounted for over 60 per cent of all retail
> trade. They employed 8 per cent of the workforce. . . . By 1992, the
> number of shopping centers had almost doubled again, and new malls
> were opening at the rate of one every seven hours. Four billion square feet
> of American landscape was shopping space, two-thirds of it built in the
> previous twenty years. . . . Mall shopping had become America's biggest
> leisure activity. . . . By the early 1990s, Americans were spending on aver-
> age twelve hours a month in shopping malls, more than they devoted to
> almost any activity other than sleeping, eating, working, and watching
> television. (Bryson 1994: 217–18)

Speaking of watching television, and especially Americans' propen-
sity to watch a lot of it, we can boost our account of everyday
ordering a good deal by considering some of the details of US televi-
sion-life Bryson puts our way. As we have already learned, by the
1990s television watching was one of the four biggest American pas-
times (along with eating, sleeping and working); but we also need to
learn that television did not rise to prominence as an ordering device
until after the Second World War. Ordering can happen very quickly,

as we have seen with our conversation and shopping examples, as well as happening over centuries, as our following sections will show. Of course, television has become one of the richest seams that Cultural Studies has mined (see especially Fishman and Cavender 1998; Fiske 1986; Fiske and Hartley 1978; Grossberg et al. 1998; Hartley 1999; McKinley 1997; Morley 1992; Williams 1974), but it seems to us that the problem with the analysis of television in Cultural Studies is the one we have already given in Chapter 1. Television is frequently associated with a kind of sinister power politics (as in the British Cultural Studies' tradition) or is analysed in terms of 'deep', 'post-modern' meanings (as in the US Cultural Studies' tradition). By contrast, our interest is in a 'shallow' analysis of television as an ordering device – we do not want to link television unproblematically to 'big politics', and we do not want to subsume television under the banner of a dizzying array of hermeneutic devices. What interests us are appearances.

As with other aspects of ordering, television works as an ordering device exactly as it itself is being ordered. After reporting on the various claims to television's invention, Bryson covers some of the early experiments – the first colour demonstration in London, by Baird, in 1928 (that is not a mistake – colour was indeed tried that early; this particular telecast featured shots of 'a man repeatedly sticking out his tongue'), and especially the first demonstration in America, in New York by Bell Telephone in 1927, on a screen 'roughly the dimensions of a modern credit card'. The broadcast (though it was hardly very broad) consisted of a speech by Herbert Hoover followed by a few Irish and 'darky' jokes told by a vaudeville comic (Bryson 1994: 228). Bryson also traces the coverage of the event by *The New York Times*, which, while marvelling at the fact that speakers in a far-off place could be heard as their lips were seen to move, nonetheless considered television's future to be limited. This prognostication may look like one of those dreadful misreadings of potential (like those, possibly mythical, instances when soft drink manufacturers turned down the chance to become licensed producers of Coca Cola because they believed the taste would not catch on), but it was correct for quite some time.

While there were 26 television stations across America by the end of 1929, only the biggest survived the next few years. 'There was no great impetus to promote the industry in America because of the lack of a market during the Great Depression and the government's refusal to allow commercials until 1941' (Bryson 1994: 229). Sales of the first sets on offer, in 1939, were poor, mainly because there was so little to watch (in America at least – the British had by this time been able to watch the BBC for ten years).

> During the war years, America had just nine television stations in five cities . . . and just seven thousand sets on which to watch the meager programming available. In the autumn of 1944, for instance, on Wednesday and Saturday nights there was no television at all in America. On Thursdays, only CBS was on the air, with fifteen minutes of news followed by an hour of local programming where available and a half-hour show called *Missus Goes a Shopping*. On Sundays the American viewer could watch DuMont Labs' *Thrills and Chills* followed by *Irwin Shane's Television Workshop*, or nothing. (Bryson 1994: 229–30)

In other words, television itself was not well enough ordered for it to play a major ordering role in people's lives. The situation changed, as is so often the case with ordering, very dramatically and almost by accident. The number of sets sold in America grew rapidly in the post-war boom, as did the sales of so many household items, and indeed the number of houses. But the big breakthrough occurred in 1948 when a programme called *Puppet Television Theater* changed its name to *Howdy Doody* and the phenomenon of the American 'TV hit' was born. With it, we suggest, was born television's capacity to organise lives: from a sometime provider of entertainment for those periods when people had nothing better to do, to an everyday provider of 'must-see' items that invited people to change their patterns of existence.

> By 1952, the number of sets had soared to eighteen million, 105 times as many as there had been just five years earlier. The seminal date for television was Monday, January 19, 1953, the date on which Lucille Ball gave birth to 'Little Ricky' on national television. (Bryson 1994: 230)

Conversing, shopping, watching television. We order ourselves and we are ordered by these and, of course, by many other activities. In a very important sense this ordering work is precisely the work of ordering the everyday, of building and maintaining a culture of everyday thinking and behaviour. However, we hardly need tell you that conversing, shopping and watching television are not usually placed at the top of any list of human endeavours which attempt to order everyday thinking and conduct. We do not need to speculate wildly to suggest that any such list drawn up for the Western world over the past 3,000 years or so would more likely be headed by items such as education, philosophy, punishment or religion. In returning to Weber and in turning to some of Paul Veyne's contributions to *The History of Private Life*, we are turning to a consideration of a combination of two of these more likely candidates to the status of guides for everyday life – religion and philosophy. But in doing so we are pointedly rejecting a 'league table' approach; for Cultural Studies as the study of ordering, all modes of ordering are worthy objects of study, as we have been at considerable pains to make clear. We turn to religion and philosophy not because they provide a better means of understanding everyday culture and the thinking and behaviour that is part of it, than do conversing, shopping and watching television – they do not – but simply because they are, in their own right, fascinating instances of this culture, yet more instances of the intricacies of ordering.

In arguing that everyday ordering crucially involves the ordering of selves, we are of course treading a ground that has been and is being explored by others, especially by a particular array of scholars influenced by some of Foucault's work (especially his 1986a and 1986b) and by some work by Pierre Hadot (1995) and Peter Brown (1988). Before proceeding to a discussion of many examples from Weber and Veyne, we acknowledge the influence upon us of Hunter (1988, 1994), McHoul and Miller (1998), T. Miller (1992), and especially Osborne (1998). We should also point out that in the next chapter we dwell upon the ordering of 'identity' through routines.

Max Weber: ordering everyday culture through religion

When we introduced you to Max Weber in an earlier chapter we were concerned with the limits of ordering. We considered Weber's *The Protestant Ethic and the Spirit of Capitalism* in terms of its historical illustrations of these limits. This text, in dealing with such matters and with others, is, of course, a rich source of examples about the role of religion in ordering everyday life. When, for example, Weber says

(1989: 36), 'the Reformation meant not the elimination of the Church's control over everyday life, but rather the substitution of a new form of control for the previous one . . . a regulation of the whole of conduct which, penetrating to all departments of private and public life, was infinitely burdensome and earnestly enforced', we are directly confronted with an example of religion attempting to order people's everyday thinking and behaviour. That these attempts could never be totally successful, as we argued in the earlier chapter's handling of Weber, is not so important to us at this juncture. Here our focus is on religion as a source of attempts to order everyday life.

Protestantism is obviously Weber's main focus, particularly the dramatic changes it brought to everyday thinking and behaviour. You will remember this quote:

> Christian asceticism . . . had, on the whole, left the naturally spontaneous character of daily life in the world untouched. Now it strode into the market-place of life, slammed the door of the monastery behind it, and undertook to penetrate just that daily routine of life with its methodicalness, to fashion it into a life in the world, but neither of nor for this world. (Weber 1989: 154)

However, to draw more from Weber on the connection between religion and attempts to control everyday activity, it is wise to look closely not just at general points about Protestantism like this one, but also at those in which Weber details the differences between Protestantism and Catholicism and the differences between Protestant sects. For instance, one of the ways he describes Calvinism is in terms of the mutual antipathy between Catholics and Calvinists. He says that while this might be explained on political grounds, more important are the 'ethical peculiarities of Calvinism' (p. 87). These 'ethical peculiarities' mark Calvinists as very different from both Lutherans and Catholics. Weber is adamant that such features of Calvinism should not be seen to be national characteristics – for example, while the Cavaliers and the Roundheads were very different types of people despite their common Englishness, no difference is easily discernible between English and German character at the end of the Middle Ages. Rather, he stresses that it was mainly religious influences 'which created the differences' between Calvinism and Catholicism and between Calvinism and other Protestant sects (pp. 88–9).

In this way, Weber lets us know that the ethical developments that are

our main interest – the capacity to influence daily thinking and conduct – were unintended consequences of the aforementioned religious
influences. He says it more directly in insisting that programmes

> of ethical reform were never at the centre of interest for any religious
> reformers. . . . They were not the founders of societies for ethical cul-
> ture. . . . The salvation of the soul and that alone was the centre of their
> life and work. . . . We shall thus have to admit that the cultural conse-
> quences of the Reformation were to a great extent . . . unforeseen and
> even unwished-for results of the labours of the reformers. (Weber
> 1989: 89–90)

Yet again we see the contingent nature of what we loosely call culture – Cultural Studies as the study of ordering insists that we try to
keep our eyes, ears and minds open to this ordering in unintended ways
that make up so much of what we call culture, and so insists that we do
not buy into any general schemas that portray culture as the surface of
some deeper force, like power and/or meaning.

Despite the importance of the religious differences mentioned above,
Weber sees some commonality: 'Above all, the types of moral conduct
in which we are interested may be found in a similar manner among the
adherents of the most various denominations' (pp. 96–7). This commonality reflects the fact that the different 'literary tools for the saving
of souls', especially 'all the casuistic compendia of the various denominations', influenced each other to the point where there are great
similarities between them even though they involved 'very great differences in actual conduct' (p. 97).

One of the major markers of this commonality was the attitude to the
possibility of an afterlife: while the 'various different dogmatic roots of
ascetic morality did no doubt die out after terrible struggles', they left
behind traces in 'undogmatic ethics' and, furthermore, we have to see
the connection of the original body of ideas with the dominant idea of
the afterlife. Without the 'power' of this idea, Weber stresses, 'no moral
awakening which seriously influenced practical life came into being in
that period' (p. 97). Weber summarises his, and our, main interest here:
'the influence of those psychological sanctions which, originating in
religious belief . . . gave a direction to practical conduct and held the
individual to it' (p. 97).

The Protestant intervention which proposed that the Church and its
rituals could have no role in determining whether an individual could
achieve a positive afterlife produced in its adherents a 'feeling of

unprecedented inner loneliness'. No priest, no God, no sacraments could help the single individual – 'forced to follow his path alone to meet his destiny which had been decreed for him'. This elimination of salvation through the Church marks the most decisive difference with Catholicism (pp. 104–5). But, more importantly for our purposes, the feeling of 'inner loneliness', as a new form of attempting to control everyday thinking, marks not just the logical conclusion of the rejection of magic – not even the burial of a loved one was to be accompanied by signs of religious ceremony – but also 'a fundamental antagonism to sensuous culture of all kinds' (p. 105).

A new mode of everyday being was born – the 'pessimistic individu-alism' that inevitably accompanied the burden of wondering about one's own predestined fate. The notion of predestination quickly began to be a major influence on people's conduct and attitudes. For instance, Weber says, it led to a lack of trust in others, even one's close friends – an important 'psychological stimulus' to the development of the Protestant ethic (p. 106). Weber suggests that it may initially seem mysterious that this isolation should lead to the superior social organ-isation of the Calvinists, but in fact, he assures us, the one definitely followed the other. For example, the dogma that acts of organisation born of brotherly love should only be undertaken for the glory of God, not because they are inherently worthy, meant that such actions assumed 'a peculiarly objective and impersonal character, that of ser-vice in the interest of the rational organization of our social environment'. Thus, 'labour in the service of impersonal social useful-ness appears to promote the glory of God and hence be willed by Him' (pp. 108–9).

Another factor in this sudden growth of this newfound everyday ordering towards organisation (towards organisational ordering, we might say) was the fact that for Calvin there was no 'conflict between the individual and the ethic' (p. 109). The spread of Calvinism was not as straightforward as it might seem – a charismatic leader easily weav-ing his doctrines – for while Calvin himself was certain he was 'a chosen agent of the Lord', this was not so easy for his followers. They became obsessed with the question of whether there are 'infallible criteria' by which the elect could be known (p. 110).

The means by which this problem was resolved gives us another dra-matic example of an unintended consequence in the story of ordering daily life. It was decided that if one could 'consider oneself chosen' one could 'combat all doubts as temptations of the devil'. The unintended consequence was that worldly activity became a means of displaying such confidence. This was possible for Calvinists because of the marked difference of Calvinism from the Lutheran *unio mystica* or 'feeling of actual absorption in the deity' (pp. 111–12). Where 'Lutheranism combines the *unio mystica* with that deep feeling of sin-stained unworthiness', the Reformed Church of Calvinism rejected this 'inward emotional piety', along with Pascal's 'Quietist escape from everything'. For the Calvinists, the human soul cannot be penetrated by the divine will, but rather God works through people and they are conscious of God's grace (p. 113). In Calvinist eyes, the religious believer is 'the tool of the divine will', not 'the vessel of the Holy Spirit'. Calvinists could not know of their status through pure feelings and emotions as these were not to be trusted. True faith could only be identified by 'conduct which served to advance the glory of God' (pp. 113–14).

So, in developing the belief that good works, while useless as a 'means of attaining salvation', are 'indispensable as a sign of election', the Calvinist created the 'conviction of his own salvation'. This is not a matter of the accumulation of good works to one's credit, as in Catholicism. Rather, it is a matter of 'systematic self-control' (p. 115).

While the Calvinist ethic may look like the Catholicism of the Middle Ages, the two are in fact very different, inasmuch as where the Catholics understood good works as part of an individual character, for Calvinists, the works were part of a 'rationalized system of life'. Catholics did not take the 'rationalization of the world' nearly so far as the Calvinists; in particular they did not reject magic to the same extent. For them, absolution was a sort of magic and their priests the magicians. Unlike the Catholics, and even the Lutherans, Calvinists could not atone for weaknesses by good will. Their God demanded 'a life of good works combined into a unified system'. They had no 'balance of merit for life as a whole'. They did not have the luxury of a 'planless and unsystematic life' (p. 117).

For the Protestant ethic, or Puritan ethic, as it was developing in the ways discussed, 'only a life guided by constant thought could achieve conquest over the state of nature' (p. 118). We suggest it is not going too far to read Weber as offering a description of the birth of a new culture of everyday life. Of course, Weber is careful to avoid the impression that this way of being and thinking emerged from thin air. It emerged as a development of certain raw materials, especially some forms of Christian asceticism in the Middle Ages which aimed at 'emancipation from planless otherworldliness and irrational self-torture' (p. 118). Puritanism took this and other types of rational asceticism, and worked them into its own attempt to achieve a controlled personality – the 'destruction of spontaneous, impulsive enjoyment' to bring order to the conduct of life (p. 119). Calvinism, in particular, differed from older forms of Christian asceticism in that it transformed them into an activity within the world (that is, the everyday world in which we operate, no matter what we are doing). Admittedly, Catholicism had tried to do this but it had never quite succeeded – ethical standards preached were seen to be 'something higher than the everyday morality which sufficed as a minimum' and, moreover, the Church's use of certain practices, especially indulgences, 'counteracted the tendencies towards systematic worldly asceticism'. Indeed, the Reformation saw this as 'one of the most fundamental evils' of the Catholic Church (p. 120).

Weber summarises much of this material by saying that the biggest difference between Calvinism and Catholicism was that the asceticism of the Catholics remained a specialist pursuit of monks while Calvinism insisted that it was much more widely practised. Luther began this process, but of course went nowhere near as far as Calvin. Calvinism took it over and extended it. Those with the most 'passionately spiritual natures' who had previously become monks were now 'forced to pursue their ascetic ideals within mundane occupations'. Calvinism thus added the necessity of 'proving one's faith in worldly activity', thereby providing a 'positive incentive to asceticism'. Through predestination, Calvinism provided grounds for a worldly division between the chosen and the damned – 'more impassable and in its invisibility more terrifying' than the division that separated monks from others in the world about them (p. 121). Weber is relentless in his search for the details of this new way of living everyday life. We think it well worth sticking with him for a while yet.

The Calvinists, he tells us, were particularly influenced by the Old Testament, especially its 'rational suppression of the mystical'. However, he stresses, this should be seen 'in the last analysis' as something stemming from the 'peculiar, fundamentally ascetic, character of Calvinism itself', not as something in the Old Testament (p. 123). In their overwhelming quest for ever-greater rationality, Calvinists copied certain Catholic orders in developing the habit of keeping 'account-books in which sins, temptations and progress' were tabulated. It almost goes without saying that they had a very different goal from that of the Catholics – where the Catholics used record-keeping to complete the confession process, the 'Reformed Christian . . . felt his own pulse with its aid' (p. 124). Later these observations were expanded to cover both the conduct of the self and that of God, seeing 'His finger in all the details of life'. Weber summarises the outcome: 'A thoroughgoing Christianization of the whole of life was the consequence of this methodical quality of ethical conduct into which Calvinism . . . forced men' (pp. 124–5).

The work done by the Calvinists via the notion of predestination was crucial not just for that sect alone, but also for Presbyterians, some Baptists and some Methodists. The central role of the idea of predestination in everyday life, Weber concludes, was the glue that held the militant reformers together during the religious strife of the seventeenth century (pp. 125–6). He goes on to discuss many of the nuances of everyday thinking and conduct generated by some of the different Protestant sects. For example, early eighteenth-century Pietism gave us the idea of 'grace gained through repentance' which had 'visible effects on conduct', particularly through Zinzendorf's interpretation which, while never strictly Pietist, pushed Pietism in an emotional direction, stressing that 'the childlikeness of religious feeling was a sign of its genuineness' (pp. 134–5).

Other features of Zinzendorf's interpretation were: repudiation of the Methodist pursuit of perfection, connected to a fundamental eudaemonistic ideal of having people experience religious bliss; commitment to missionary work and hence to labour in a calling; 'dislike of philosophical speculation as dangerous to faith' and a consequent commitment to empirical knowledge (p. 136). 'All in all', Weber summarises, German Pietism was weaker than 'the iron consistency of Calvinism', such that self-confidence in a calling was overshadowed by 'an attitude of humility' (p. 137). He traces this to the Lutheran notion of salvation and forgiveness of sins. Pietism, he says, was concerned with promoting the virtues of 'the faithful official, clerk, labourer, or domestic worker', where Calvinism was concerned with 'the hard legalism and active enterprise of bourgeois-capitalistic entrepreneurs' (pp. 138–9).

Another sect which attempted to combine emotional with ascetic Protestantism, but with a stronger emphasis on systematic conduct, was Anglo-American Methodism. Wesley's Methodism saw its mission among the masses, and the emotional 'struggles' involved were crucial. A peculiar alliance with ascetic ethics was involved. For Methodism, the certainty of salvation derived from 'the testimony of the spirit, the coming of which could be definitely placed to the hour'. To this Wesley added the doctrine of sanctification, whereby one reborn in this manner could achieve sanctification even in this life (pp. 139–40). For Wesley, good works were 'not the cause but only the means of know-ing one's state of grace'. Rather, to attain true grace, one had to seek 'sudden emotional transformation', however difficult it was to achieve (he thought it would not be usually until late in one's life). Methodists thereby introduced into this already heady brew of everyday culture a conflict between the possibility of sudden grace and the, until this time unchallenged, idea of predestination (p. 141). However, the Protestant 'revolution' in everyday thinking and conduct was not disturbed – the maintenance of 'aspiration to the higher life' served as a 'sort of makeshift' for predestination (pp. 142–3). Methodism remained essen-tially Calvinistic – the emotional enthusiasm was occasional and it 'by no means destroyed the otherwise rational character of conduct' (p. 143).

So far we have been using Weber suggestively – allowing you to draw your own connections between, on the one hand, the remarkable shifts in modes of everyday being made possible by the rise of Protestantism and, on the other, modern everyday thinking and con-duct, including perhaps the thinking and behaviour involved in conversing, shopping and watching television. To conclude our treat-ment of Weber's text we consider some examples of the connections he draws between Protestant everyday conduct and attitudes and the development of certain everyday conduct and attitudes seen as neces-sary for, or at least highly beneficial to, the spread of capitalism, understood as a way of economic life.

The Baptists, he tells us, 'repudiated all idolatry of the flesh, as a detraction from the reverence due to God alone'. They organised their daily lives in the belief that God always had more to reveal and that He would speak, through the Holy Spirit, 'to any individual who is willing to hear'. Some Baptists, especially the Quakers, even 'did away with . . . the sole authority of the Bible'. In setting up their extreme religious rationalisation all sacraments were devalued – only inner reflection could allow one truly to understand the Bible: hence their idea of the invisible Church. All Baptists aimed at having a 'pure' Church – featuring the 'blameless conduct of their members'. Their rationalisation of daily life was based not on predestination, but on patient waiting for the Spirit to descend – 'silent waiting . . . to overcome everything irrational and impulsive, the passions and subjective interests'. Even in later Baptist movements – particularly, again, the Quakers – the rejection of political life meant a turn *to* worldly asceticism, not a turn away from the world; the elimination of magic from the world 'allowed no other psychological course' (pp. 146–9). This is an extreme example of the unintended consequence at the heart of Weber's book: the Baptists' reformulation of the culture of everyday life fitted them perfectly for the everyday life of the capitalist. Another factor which makes the Baptists so significant for Weber's study is the fact that their rejection of politics, in turning their attention inwards, produced their conscientiousness in governing their own conduct, which in turn led to an ethic of 'honesty is the best policy', which in turn proved so suitable to the development of capitalism (p. 151).

Moving to a slightly earlier era, Weber says he uses the writings of the seventeenth-century English minister Richard Baxter, who, remarkably, served both Cromwell's parliamentary government and the Restoration government, as exemplary of Puritan ethics. Baxter focused on wealth and acquisition, seeing great danger in wealth. On close examination, Weber tells us, while Baxter was much more concerned about wealth and possessions than was Calvin, his objections were to do not with wealth *per se*, but solely with the fact that wealth and possessions inevitably led to idleness and to a slackening of work in the calling. 'Waste of time is thus the first and . . . deadliest of sins.' Baxter, in promoting 'hard, continuous bodily or mental labour', opposes too much sleep, too much contemplation (only something for Sundays), and any sex, even within marriage, which is not for the purpose of procreation (pp. 156–8).

Baxter's commitment to the idea of labour in the calling as an end in itself was much stronger than a similar commitment in medieval theology. He did not, for example, think the wealthy were exempt. This subtle difference 'had far-reaching psychological consequences'. Where Aquinas and Luther saw the division of labour as a matter of fortune or God's will, for the Puritans it was a much more important and relevant matter. Indeed, Baxter was not too far from Adam Smith in believing that increases in production, and thus in the common wealth, are good for everyone. His twist however was that this has to be done in a regular and methodical way, and that irregular work, even if it led to an increase in production, could not be more than a transition. The calling was what was most important (pp. 159–61).

The significance of these ethical subtleties for the development of 'economic selves' and economic organisation more generally are not difficult to see. Baxter's consistent approach to the worth of labour in a calling, for example, allowed people to pursue more than one calling at a time and/or to change callings, provided that the change was considered to be for the good of the community or the self in the sight of God. In line with this, it was not only reasonable, but desirable that the elect should make a profit, again provided it was done in line with God's direction. The goal of person formation was 'the sober, middle-class, self-made man'. To be avoided were laziness, begging, wanting to be poor, as well as ostentatious displays of wealth (pp. 162–3).

The general 'inner attitude' of the English Puritans, Weber argues, was one of 'thankfulness for one's own perfection', an attitude which 'played its part in developing that formalistic, hard, correct character which was peculiar to the men of that heroic age of capitalism'. This asceticism 'turned with all its force against one thing: the spontaneous enjoyment of life and all it had to offer'. This is exemplified in the considerable struggle which ensued in the early sixteenth century between the Crown and the Puritans over sport. James I and Charles I made *The Book of Sports* into law, allowing certain sports on Sundays, to counteract the anti-authoritarian asceticism of the Puritans. The Puritans, it should be remembered, were not opposed to sport *per se*, only to its playing for spontaneous pleasure instead of as 'recreation necessary for physical efficiency' (pp. 166–7).

In a similar vein, the Puritans were more than accepting of science, but did not accept higher learning if it took the form of arts and literature. Only in Holland did a Puritan art exist and this only in the ascetic guise of realism. The theatre and any adornment of dress were also frowned upon, although we should remember there were contradictions. Any tolerance for pleasure in worldly goods, or in artistic or sporting pursuits, was severely limited, in any case, by the requirement that they should cost nothing: part of the Puritan ethic was a commitment to account for every penny to ensure that nothing was spent on possessions which did not increase the glory of God; only possessions which did so were considered worthy (pp. 168–70). One consequence of this attitude to possessions was that it encouraged careful acquisition; the 'solid comfort of the middle-class home' became an ideal. This ethos of honest, disciplined, careful acquisition whereby wealth for its own sake was frowned upon but wealth for the glory of God was encouraged was a boon for the spirit of capitalism: 'accumulation of capital through ascetic compulsion to save' (pp. 171–2).

The great religious upheavals of the seventeenth century, Weber reminds us, gradually gave way to a situation in which, first, it was acceptable to 'have the best of both worlds', that is, to acquire wealth in this world in the certainty of gaining a place in the next, and second it was acceptable to pursue a middle-class existence provided one did so honestly and with a good conscience. In other words, religion slowly lost its importance as a part of the ethic of capitalism. The bourgeois businessman was thus able to go about his wealth creation comfortable in the knowledge that he was fulfilling a duty in so doing. He was even able to justify inequalities of wealth on the grounds that these inequalities were ordained by God, that the God-ordained poverty which goes with them was crucial to discipline the workers (pp. 176–7).

An extreme instance of this sanctioning of poverty was the involvement of the English Puritans in drawing up the harsh Poor Laws. Despite this, Protestant asceticism encouraged the loyalty of the low-paid workers by providing a psychological sanction through the idea of labour in a calling, as the best, perhaps only, means to attain salvation. In England the Puritans rejected the Laud – an alliance of Church and State which allowed the formation of monopolistic commercial enterprises – in favour of enterprise based solely on merit and sober industry. It was their shopkeepers' mentality which became the true spirit of capitalism: 'rational conduct on the basis of the idea of the calling, was born' (pp. 178–80).

Weber summarises the differences between this position and early-twentieth-century possibilities when he says:

> The Puritan wanted to work in a calling; we are forced to do so. For when asceticism was carried out of the monastic cells into everyday life, and began to dominate worldly morality, it did its part in building the tremendous cosmos of the modern economic order. This order is now bound to the technical and economic conditions of machine production which to-day

determine the lives of all the individuals who are born into this mechanism. . . . Since asceticism undertook to remodel the world and to work out its ideals in the world, material goods have gained an increasing and finally an inexorable power over the lives of men as at no previous period in history'. (p. 181)

Despite the rigour with which Weber takes us suddenly forward to the twentieth century, we do not mean in any way to suggest by our borrowings from him that the great religious changes of sixteenth- and seventeenth-century Europe are a cause, however far removed, of things like the capacity of modern Americans (and other Westerners) to own and to enjoy watching televisions and to shop for a vast array of other consumer goods. Our method, of course, does not encourage such causal thinking (something we devote much more space to in Kendall and Wickham 1999). But, in focusing on appearances, their systematisations and their uses, our method does encourage us to consider the way the uses and systematisations of appearances involve existing uses and systematisations – what we, in our Foucaultian way, sometimes call conditions of possibility. In other words, where the appearances of conversing, shopping and watching television we presented earlier in this chapter might be used and systematised into accounts of everyday life offered by dominant modes of Cultural Studies as somehow caused by systems of power and meaning, we are suggesting that they be thought of, instead, as appearances of ordering, thereby systematising and using them in terms of the uses and systematisations of everyday ordering offered by Weber and Paul Veyne, to whom we now turn our attention.

Paul Veyne: ordering culture through religion and philosophy

The details we borrow from Veyne demonstrate the longevity of certain cultural techniques for attempting to order everyday life by ordering the self. Of course every technique must be considered in its own right and, it almost goes without saying, we share the passion displayed by Weber and Veyne for marking differences, but nonetheless we are comfortable with the level of generality required for the following claim (comfortable enough so that we have kept making it throughout the book): to study culture through studying ordering, one should always seek to gather evidence of the appearances of attempts at ordering; be aware of their diversity by all means, and of attempts to systematise and use them, but do not lose sight of the fact that to gather them as evidence is in itself the central part of such study.

We begin our coverage of Veyne's contribution with a point of difference. He says his account of everyday life in the Roman Empire in pagan times is meant to offer 'sufficient detail' to bring out the 'dramatic contrast with Christianization' (Veyne 1992: 1). Going further in qualifying/clarifying mode, in answer to his own questions, 'Why begin with the Romans? Why not the Greeks?' Veyne speaks of the power of Hellenistic civilisation in Roman times – 'a universal civilization (universal for that time, at any rate) spanned the territory from Gibraltar to the Indus: Hellenistic civilization. The Romans, a marginal people, managed to conquer this territory and complete their own Hellenization' (p. 2). He goes on: 'Rome adopted as its own the culture of another nation, Greece. . . . Thus, this volume begins by describing private life in the Empire that is called Roman but might just as well be called Hellenic' (p. 3).

Veyne emphasises the fact that the division between religion and philosophy was not what it would later become. He says that for both philosophy and religion in the Roman world, the crucial question was 'How can individual anxieties about life be alleviated?' There was not, he stresses, any particular interest in the hereafter.

> Indeed, the very existence of a hereafter was often denied, or else the other world was such a vague concept that it implied little more than the peacefulness of death, the tranquility of the grave. Philosophy, religion and the afterlife aroused precious little anxiety. What is more, the boundaries of their respective provinces were so unlike what they are today that the three words meant something quite different from what we imagine. Who am I? What should I do? Where am I headed, and have I any reason for hope? There is nothing natural about these modern questions; they derive from their Christian answers. Ancient religion and philosophy managed to get along without asking them. (Veyne 1992: 207)

Where philosophy in the modern world is an 'academic subject' and religion is 'an amalgam of spiritual practices, moral precepts, and thoughts about the afterlife',

> For the ancients . . . moral precepts and spiritual practices were an essential part of 'philosophy', rather than religion, which had very little to do with

ideas about death and the hereafter. Sects existed, but they were philosophical sects. . . . One became a Stoic or an Epicurean and lived more or less faithfully, according to the convictions of one's sect – much as one might become a Christian or a Marxist today. (Veyne 1992: 207)

In terms of everyday conduct, Veyne suggests, the situation in ancient Rome was more like that which prevails in 'modern Japan, where a man can take an interest in a Buddhist sect, yet still observe, like everyone else, Shinto religious practices', than it was like the modern Western situation (p. 208). As we keep saying, the culture of everyday ordering is complex and shifting. Nothing can be taken for granted. All details must be respected.

Concentrating on religion, Veyne says, 'The paganism of the Greeks and Romans, though a religion without salvation or afterlife, was not necessarily indifferent to man's moral behavior.' It 'was more an à la carte religion than a religion with a fixed menu. If an established church is a "one-party state", then paganism was "free-enterprise". Each man was free to found his own temple and preach whatever god he liked, just as he might open an inn or peddle a new product' (p. 208); (so, the episode of *The Simpsons* in which Homer decides to start his own religion is not so fanciful after all, and nor, for that matter, is the opening scene of Monty Python's *Life of Brian*, in which people wander about declaiming their individual religions in the manner of 'political visionaries').

Where the idea of God for Christians, Jews and Moslems relates to a supreme being – 'He exists solely as an actor in a cosmic drama in which the salvation of humankind is played out' – the 'pagan gods, by contrast, live their lives and are not confined to a metaphysical role' (p. 208). Veyne here seems to be telling us that the Romans practised what we would call religious toleration, but from a different base. Where modern everyday thinking may see wisdom in a 'live and let live' policy for practical reasons born of knowledge of the havoc religious intolerance can wreak, the Romans believed that 'the gods of all peoples are true gods' as a part of their ontology. Their gods 'are part of this world, one of three races that inhabit the earth: animals, which are neither immortal nor gifted with reason; humans, who are mortal but reasonable; and gods, who are immortal and reasonable' (p. 208). In line with this, the relations 'between men and their deities resembled relations between ordinary men and such powerful brethren as kings or patrons'. Sometimes this involved flattering the gods, sometimes being suspicious of them, sometimes even trying to wear them down (p. 210).

Piety lay not in faith, works, or contemplation but in a whole range of practices that seem self-interested only because the beloved god-patron was a protector. Illness, travel, and childbirth were occasions to prove one's loyal confidence in one's protector. . . . Detailed and complex, religious rites were performed with great care in a meditative spirit. . . . If we knew nothing of the pleasure pagans took in performing these rites, we could no more understand . . . sculptures [which depict them] than an asexual being can understand an erotic film. . . . The tranquilizer of magic was hardly distinguishable from the tranquilizer of religion. (Veyne 1992: 211–13)

Religion for the Romans also served as an 'impartial guarantor of a system of ethics and interests that wished to appear disinterested', although Veyne stresses that it did not play this role as well as philosophy played it. 'The gods' intervention was recognized and anticipated only where laudable and desirable, and no attention was paid to anything else' (p. 214).

Turning to the question of attitudes towards religion, especially 'whether, for an educated person, it was ridiculous, beneath contempt', Veyne notes that 'culture' for the Romans meant '"to be cultivated" . . . "not [to] think like the common folk". Culture was a privilege, along with wealth and power.' He goes on to suggest that religion was something of a 'cultural divide'. Cicero, for instance, regarded religion as 'an amalgam of foolish superstitions, good for the uneducated' (p. 217). This began to change, Veyne argues, around AD 100. At this time paganism

ceased to be a mythological religion and began to prefigure the Christian relation to God. Relations between men and gods ceased to be those between two living species . . . and became those between a monarch and his subjects. This monarch was either a single, providential god or a collection of providential gods. . . . They lost their mythical biography and personal traits. All fulfilled the same function: to govern, counsel, and protect men and rescue them from the grip of blind Fortune or Fate. (Veyne 1992: 218)

The Romans devoted little thought or attention, as we have already glimpsed, to the question of the afterlife.

The Epicureans did not believe in the immortality of the soul, Stoics did not much believe in it, and official religion for the most part avoided the question. . . . The most widely held opinion, even among the lower orders, was that death is nothingness, eternal sleep. (Veyne 1992: 219)

And what of philosophy? For the ancients, the aim of philosophy was not, as it later was for Kant,

> establishing the possible grounds for morality. The aim of ancient philosophy was to provide individuals with a method for obtaining happiness. A sect was not a school where people came to learn general ideas; they came looking for rational means of achieving tranquility. (Veyne 1992: 223)

Morality featured only as a possible means to this end, not as an end in itself.

> The Epicurean and Stoic sects offered adherents a formula based on the nature of the universe . . . whose purpose was to enable them to live without fear of men, gods, chance, or death, to make individual happiness independent of accidents of fate . . . to make men as tranquil as the gods, their mortal equals. The differences between the two sects lay in subtleties, and in the metaphysics used to justify their remedies. (Veyne 1992: 223)

More importantly, for our quest for evidence about everyday ordering,

> Both sects were contemptuous not only of death but also of vain desires, desires for money and honors, perishable goods that cannot promise unbreachable security. . . . Both sects held that a man who, because of illness or persecution, found it impossible to lead a humane life in his body or his city could reasonably resort to suicide; indeed, suicide was the recommended remedy in such situations. (Veyne 1992: 224)

This was the case to the extent that 'the suicide proved the truth of the philosophical notion that what matters is the quality and not the quantity of the time that one lives' (p. 229).

'The sects did not barrage their members with moral precepts; they promised happiness. . . . Stoicism and Epicureanism were intellectual faiths' (p. 224). And as with other faiths, a crucial aspect of the sects was their commitment to propaganda through polemic (it was the sects who first made use of words such as 'dogma', 'heresy' and 'conversion'; the Christians merely inherited these terms). While every sect – Stoicism, Epicureanism, Platonism, Cynicism, Pythagoreanism, to name just some – 'continued the doctrine of its founder and remained, or believed that it remained, faithful to his dogmas', nonetheless, the 'idea of an unfettered search for the truth was anathema . . . each sect engaged in ardent polemic with its rivals' (p. 227).

But whatever the sects got up to, we must remember that their main role was the ordering of everyday lives:

> As Pierre Hadot has shown, an ancient philosophy was not constructed to be interesting or true but to be put into practice, to change lives, and to be profoundly assimilated through intellectual exercises, which serve as the model for the spiritual exercises of Christianity. These exercises were to be practised every day. . . . Members were supposed to meditate upon the sect's dogmas and apply them to everyday events. . . . Private life took refuge in self-mastery, in both senses of the term: having the strength to control the course of one's life, and granting oneself the sovereign privilege to do so rather than leaving the decision to nature or to a god. (Veyne 1992: 228)

By way of comparison, Veyne says later societies saw private life very differently:

> In other societies private life later came to mean secession from public life, or sailing life's seas as a solitary mariner – or a pirate – tossed by the winds of individual desire, fancy, and fantasy. It [was] narcissistic and self-indulgent [for the Greeks and Romans] to give free rein to desire, fancy, and fantasy. . . . Tranquility was bought at the price of tension and renunciation – hallmarks of the ancient world as much as of the world of the samurai or of Queen Victoria. (Veyne 1992: 229)

In line with this, deliberately to seek experience was a practice much frowned upon by the ancients. In this sense, they seem to have ordered themselves quite differently from many modern Westerners:

> As Heidegger says, the Greeks went to the games at Olympia because they were interesting and an institution. None of them said, 'This is an experience I absolutely must have'. Indeed, to want to explore the unknown was considered a vicious temptation, something to be feared, and was called 'curiosity'. This was the vice to which those who indulged in magic were prone, and it always ended badly. (Veyne 1992: 230–1)

Veyne develops this theme by telling us that the Greeks and Romans had no interest in talking in depth about their own selves. While the figure 'I' might appear in Greek and Roman poetry, this usage was only like that employed in modern pop songs:

> The modern singer and the ancient poet do not recount their loves and sorrows; rather they set Jealousy and Love on a stage. . . . To talk about oneself, to throw personal testimony into the balance, to profess that personal conviction must be taken into account provided only that it is sincere

is a Christian, indeed an eminently Protestant idea that the ancients never dared to profess. (Veyne 1992: 231–2)

Conclusion

So goes the ordering of daily life – so complex we should not hope to find too many instances exactly the same, yet so widespread in time and space we can find fascinating similarities mingling with fascinating differences. We believe we have given you ample opportunity to see this for yourselves through our account of the culture of everyday ordering. We began this chapter with a discussion of how conversation is an ordering technique; various conversational gambits are 'programmatic' to the extent that they invite certain sorts of responses, and seek to lay down the rules for how the future will unfold. To engage in conversation is to take part in the world of ordering. Following on from this, we discussed two 'everyday' ordering devices: shopping malls and television. Shopping malls provide an architecture, a space which is simultaneously liberating and constraining, giving shape to our lives but also inventing new possibilities. Similarly, television orders, limits, and suggests: on the one hand, it has given us a multitude of new possibilities, insights into new parts of the world and ways of doing things; on the other, it organises and closes down (at the very least, we are probably all aware of the way in which television schedules impact on the organisation of daily life, influencing and ordering such decisions as when we eat and when we go to sleep). Television has also been linked with one aspect of globalisation, specifically the spread of a homogeneous (Americanised) culture; our emphasis is much more on the heterogeneity of television's ordering – orderings are plural, rather than singular.

Next, we discussed Weber's famous work on religion as a factor in the formation of a certain type of personality. What is especially important here is that we take from Weber the contingency that surrounds these forms of ordering of the self. Once again, culture provides a series of 'programmes' (Latour 1987), but these programmes do not have to be taken up, and are frequently refused, partially accepted, revised and mangled. What this suggests to us is that a sceptical description of appearances is the proper limit of investigation.

Finally, we expounded upon Paul Veyne's descriptions of antique private life. The forms of self that Veyne describes are barely recognisable to us, and it is important that we do not allow ourselves to somehow render the ancient experience comparable to our own. We must let the details stand and speak for themselves. These details form an ordering web; fragile, temporary, contingent, relational. Their meanings are given by their order, rather than vice versa.

We give the last word to the wonderful Georges Perec, this time talking about the everyday problem of ordering books. We are sure you will know just what he means:

> In my own case, nearly three-quarters of my books have never really been classified. Those that are not arranged in a definitely provisional way are arranged in a provisionally definite way. . . . Meanwhile, I move them from one room to another, one pile to another, and may spend three hours looking for a book without finding it but sometimes having the satisfaction of coming upon six or seven others which serve my purpose just as well. (Perec 1997: 149–50)

7 Ordering Through Routinisation – Technique, Technology and Self

One of the issues which began to come into focus in the previous chapter was 'identity'. Identity is a staple concern of Cultural Studies. On the one hand, it is often characterised as constructed by dominant power mechanisms for their own nefarious purposes; on the other hand, identity can be seen as a point of resistance which sits outside those mechanisms. Identity (especially subcultural identity – see for example, Frith 1988; Hayward 1992; Hebdige 1979) is frequently celebrated as a possible avenue of escape from the logic of capitalism. Nowhere has this tendency been more marked than in the field of popular culture, which has been treated as the realm of the 'authentic' (usually working-class) refusal of the meanings and values that the dominant orders would impose. One of the jobs we take on in this chapter is to argue against the concept of identity: it is a flabby, ill-defined concept which cannot satisfy our demands for precision and detail. Before we do that, we need to do some groundwork for our refusal of identity, and this is done by a discussion of technique and technology. This discussion is mapped on to a discussion of the self as fluid / disordered or fixed / routinised / ordered. Later, we move on to discussing the actor-networks of Bruno Latour as the ordered spaces where the self and other roles can exist. Latour allows us to replace the notion of identity with an attention to the routinisation of a network which includes, but is not limited to, human actors. By the end, we hope we have managed to undermine the notion of 'identity' – so central to a Cultural Studies which wishes to travel endlessly across the wastelands of power and meaning – and replaced it with an attention to the self as a component in more or less routinised network. The self, then, is rendered emergent and relational in our analysis, but we shall not be able to describe it unless we can describe those routinisations: those orderings.

The self as a technical achievement

A long line of sociologists has argued that the self is contingent, transitory, piecemeal, and, above all, *technical*. By technical, we mean that the self is simply an agglomeration of 'techniques' for doing things. This perspective has perhaps been most famously suggested by Marcel Mauss (see, for example, 1973); Mauss described some of the various 'techniques of the body' that are used in different societies at different historical conjunctures, stressing, importantly, their contingent form. For Mauss, there is no truly or simply human way of walking, eating or swimming, for example. In similar vein, Elias (1978) dealt with the formation of the person of the Renaissance courtier: the courtier does not build up a coherent form of selfhood based on some *telos*, but merely takes elements from here and there, as they are pleasing and useful. The self is a temporary aggregation of these 'pleasing ways', but not especially systematic or coherent: rather it is emergent and contingent. In the later Foucault (especially 1986b; Martin et al. 1988), too, we see an analysis of the self as 'technical', and the emergence of a new vocabulary which stresses 'techniques of the self' and 'technologies of the self'. Foucault (unlike most post-Foucaultians) does discriminate carefully between these two terms, using the French *technique* to refer to a practical *instance*, while the term *technologie* refers to a practical *system*. In a nut-shell, techniques are singular and elemental, while technologies are accretions of techniques formed into a logical and systematic whole. When we think of this vocabulary as applied to the object 'the self', a technique of the self is a skill or procedure, possibly isolated or possibly integrated with other techniques; a technology of the self, by contrast, is something much more like a Wittgensteinian 'form of life' or a Weberian 'department of existence'.

Foucault made use of antique notions in formulating his work on technique and technology. The Greeks did not use a word equivalent to 'technology' to describe forms of activity or creation. The Greek term *techne* (plural *technai*) is closer to our term 'technique', but should be carefully discriminated from it. A *techne* refers to any skill or ability. Etymologically it is connected to the word for 'weaving' and, further down the road of derivation, to the word for a 'text', a thing that has been woven together out of words. The Greeks, then, have a very physical and, one may say, organic view of the *technai*. They are understood as practical, rather than mental, applications. A technique of the self (or *techne heautou*), then, is not simply a reflective sense of self but a lived and practical experience. We must bear this in mind when we read Foucault: the sense of self he is talking about is nothing like the modern idea of the reflective, intellectual self divorced from the realm of the body, but rather a self formed from the playing out of ways of comporting oneself in the *bios politikos*, public life.

It is worth stressing that what we wish to take from Foucault, contrary to almost all other Anglophone readings, is the notion of uniqueness: that is, every technique has its own conditions of possibility, every technique has its own specificity. We are much less interested, at least for the moment, in 'technologies' – organised, coherent sets of techniques.

From technique to socio-technological systems

Now we move on to discuss the realm described by Bruno Latour as the 'socio-technological' – the realm where human and non-human (technological) actors live and work together. Latour's (1992, 1993, 1999) critique of sociology (and the other social sciences) targets the way in which it proceeds by ignoring the natural and technological actors (or 'actants', as Latour terms them, borrowing from the linguist A.J. Greimas) that are necessary for any social situation to work. Together with his colleague Michel Callon, Latour has pointed to the role of natural actants (scallops, yeast), technological actants (car seat belts, automatic doors) and social actants (humans, corporations) – but for Latour the distinctions between these types of actants are problematic. Just as for John Law, as we saw in Chapter 3 for Latour it is possible to understand attributions of differences between actors as a *result* of networks rather than their starting point. Further, Latour insists that a social analysis must encompass the sorts of actants we have previously been at pains to exclude from our inquiries.

It is not our intention at this point to gloss Latour's work any further, but when we return to Foucault's 'technologies of the self', what should be apparent is that there is really no technology in them – there is little attention to the routinised chains that connect the human and the non-human. Foucault's self is purely human and purely social, but Latour would direct us to the fact that we never see human beings in such purely human and/or social settings. Humans are always enmeshed in a network with other actants, many of which are non-humans (humans driving cars, wearing clothes and spectacles, carrying mobile phones, and so forth). And while our twenty-first-century human being is clearly simultaneously human, natural, social, technological, etc., the same argument *mutatis mutandis* can be made for the ancients – and here we can say that Foucault's emphasis on the antique does not provide an excuse for ignoring the non-human. The challenge here is to conceptualise a form of self that encompasses and includes the technological. For example, as we sit at our desks and write this chapter, we are ordered and constrained at the same time as our thoughts are liberated by Apple Macintosh™, Microsoft Word™, the internet facilities that allow us to work together over distances of thousands of miles, the tables and chairs at which we sit, the layout, heating and air-conditioning of our offices, the social rules about when it is appropriate to work, university authorities' attempts to increase published output, our publisher's deadlines, and so forth. A technology of the self must simultaneously apprehend all of these dimensions: social, natural, and technological and, importantly, their sometime systematicity.

Uniqueness and systematicity

In comparing Latour and Foucault, we can make the following observations. Foucault's sensitivity to uniqueness – the *ad hoc* method that arises in isolation (technique) and may or may not cohere with other techniques to produce a system (a technology) seems a particularly useful counterpoint to Latour's emphasis upon the systemic and routinised. Of course, for Latour the emergence of systems or networks is constantly being reproduced moment by moment, and this entails *ad hoc* (or what we might term 'technical') processes.

Nevertheless, as we have seen, Latour stresses systematicity – the tying together of actors through the movements of intermediaries which must be more or less routinised if a network is to be successfully put together and operate durably. We see this most clearly in Latour's ascription to particular technological artefacts (that is, those techno-logical artefacts that are embedded within material-semiotic systems) the status of 'missing masses' that serve in the reproduction of social order. While this emphasis upon the process of ordering seems one-sided, it does supplement Foucault by injecting technology more forcefully as an actor in the process of 'caring for the self', of 'govern-mentality', of discipline and so on. And the reader should note the precise terms that we use here to convey the force of Latour's thought – it dwells on the 'technological' (the systematic, routinised, enframing) rather than the technical (the singular, the discrete, the *ad hoc*).

If we take these two contributions together, we can embrace the rela-tion between uniqueness and systematicity: let us call those technological artefacts involved in this double movement of uniqueness and systematicity 'artefactual non-humans' (to distinguish them from the dichotomy of technique/technology). We can begin to trace how 'artefactual non-humans' are complex distributions, relationalities and assemblages, which are systematised and yet which are also moments of uniqueness and novelty. They serve in processes of ordering and disordering.

Michael (2000: 112–4) gives us an example to help us think through this issue. Let us take his example of the 'artefactual non-human' known as the television remote control. Clearly, this can be regarded as a com-ponent in the socio-technological system or network that includes at minimum the television, TV companies and manufacturers, consumers, infra-red light. However, the remote control is liable to be lost. As Michael argues, this is due in part to a coincidentalisation of technolo-gies – in particular the consonance in the designs of the remote control and the sofa (or couch). What makes this consonance possible are struc-turing assumptions concerning the hand (the remote is designed to fit into one; the sofa is designed to allow the hand entry for removal of cushions, opening of sofa beds, etc.). As such, a pathway is opened whereby the remote control can get lost. The response to this occa-sional breakdown in the socio-technical system (in which the remote control is embedded) is the local innovation of new, more or less unique strategies – that is, techniques – that guard against such loss. For instance, the remote control can be systematically located in some 'safe' place after use. However, these strategies can also reflect more systemic conditions such as familial relations. To the extent that such relations are partly mediated by the father's monopoly of the remote control (cf. Morley 1992), it may well be the arm of the father's chair on which the remote regularly and safely settles. Further, such mishaps also come to be articulated and fixed by more 'global' socio-technical actors: thus Philips produces Magnavox Remote Locator™ colour televisions which help TV viewers swiftly locate their lost remote controls by pressing the TV's 'Power-On' button.

This example suggests that certain engagements with technology as materials lead to disorder (the missing remote, the lumpy sofa), points of change (a realignment of viewers and viewing from the floor to the chair), new ordering relationships (as the battle for rights to use the technology is joined), further points of change (new technologies are invented to deal with the existing socio-technical problem), and so forth. This allows us to focus on the moments of transition where technique becomes technology (the individual, *ad hoc* problem turns into a routinised solution – from the lost remote control to the Magnavox Remote Locator™), and technology technique (the forms of routinisation themselves develop *ad hoc*, singular problems – from the useful device which saves us having to get up and go to the television set to change channels to the useless device stuck down the side of the sofa). In this way, we can go beyond the lexical slippage between the two terms to suggest that when considered as a pair, technique and technology – that is as 'artefactual non-humans' – allow us to apprehend uniqueness, materiality, change and ordering. All of these elements exist in the space between the practical instances of techniques and the practical systems of technologies.

As a second example, we might consider Kendall's (1999) discussion of music technology and music production. Kendall is keen to dismiss those (sadly ubiquitous) perspectives which dismiss 'hi-tech' music as 'soulless', inferior, robotic and inhuman. Such perspectives ignore Latour's insistence on symmetry (as discussed in Chapter 3) by according different values to actants in the network. In this case, the authoritative, authorial humans are wrongly prioritised over their accomplices, the machines and instruments with which music is composed, produced and disseminated. The production of music out of a network of diverse actants – natural, technological, human – can only be accomplished once the network has attained a (temporary) order, once it is routinised enough that it can begin to be productive. By themselves, human beings cannot make music that can be transported to and heard in other times and places – they require non-human intermediaries to produce a flexible, transportable, durable artefact. So, humans need the instruments that both constrain and liberate 'creativity'. These instruments suggest certain actions ('programmes'), although it is possible that other actions ('anti-programmes') may come into existence – thus it makes little sense to locate 'creativity' solely within human actants. For example, in 1982 Roland, a leading electronic musical instrument manufacturer, manufactured and marketed the TB-303, a machine designed to emulate a human bass player. The programme Roland put to work is clear: 'buy this machine and use it as a substitute for a human playing a bass guitar'. However, no doubt partly because the TB-303 sounded nothing like a human playing a bass guitar, some musicians launched an anti-programme, and used the TB-303 to produce the squeals, pulses and filter sweeps characteristic of 'acid house' music. In these instances of creativity, we can see a complex relation between the programme and the anti-programme, and we can see that the creation of a new musical genre and its associated compositions required actants of all types – natural, human and technological.

And it is not just the instruments that our humans require: they also need to record, preserve and distribute their music (on to cassette or digital audio-tape or reel-to-reel or compact disc or mini-disc), and without friendly and helpful non-human co-actants, no music would ever be heard anywhere but in a singular instance of time and space (the actual time and location of the performance).

Of course, it is possible to argue that human beings are the originary point of any form of creativity. You, the reader, may well agree that human beings require other actants, including the non-human, to produce something durable, movable and listenable to; but surely human beings can be isolated from the routinised technological systems and held up as the *fons et origo* of the network? Absolutely not. Kendall makes use of Hirst and Woolley (1982) to argue that the human being has never been 'pure', and has always been a hybrid. Hirst and Woolley's point is that tool use is not so much a description of one of the characteristics of *homo sapiens*, it is a condition of possibility for the evolution of *homo sapiens*. What this means, if one wants a snappy motto, is that the human being is always-already technological; by this we mean that the human being is always-already enmeshed within a routinised, contingent, fragile, (temporarily) ordered network. There is no *a priori* moment at which we can identify a pure, non-hybridised human. Hence, if we still wish to accord a driving role to a single actant in a network (and usually this would be the human actant), we shall find that that human is 'impure'. The cyborg has already arrived – almost unnoticed, and in situations far removed from science fiction (see also Haraway 1991).

Against identity

In Cultural Studies, as we have already seen, the term 'identity' is used frequently (and carelessly) to refer to some sense of self, and especially to a self-reflective sense of self, and perhaps to a self which can stand against mechanisms of power/the logic of capitalism/insert your favoured 'conspiracy' term here. Michel Serres (1998) has reflected on a basic problem with the use of this term which serves as a useful starting point for our discussion here. Serres, as a mathematician, draws attention to the literal meaning of the term 'identity': an exact equivalence between two entities, statements or symbols. The identity of 'x' is, of course 'x'; 'x' may be identical with 'y', but we would then know that there would not be much point in using separate symbols for them; or a transformation of one object may render it identical with another $(2x + c = y)$. When one transfers this kind of understanding to the use of the term 'identity' in Cultural Studies, one can see the problem; most of the time in Cultural Studies, the notion of identity is used to link two entities which are far from identical (as in 'person x's identity is that s/he is a y', or, more simply, 'x is a y'). The problem here is that we are imposing identity when person x merely belongs (and probably not exclusively) to the set of entities named y.

This is not trivial: it suggests that the way we typically understand identity (and hence *a fortiori* identity politics) is to engage in a process of over-extension and simplification. In fact, it is almost impossible to designate that which is identical with person x (that is to say, to designate all the qualities of which person x partakes); logically, it may only be possible to say something which is a truism – person x is person x.

Interestingly enough, the opposite logical problem may also point up a problem for 'identity': frequently the term is used to fix two entities that are not identical. Person x may be said to have an identity as, say, a heterosexual black woman – yet it is clearly the case that no form of 'identity' is evident. However, such uses of the term identity allow the commentator, as if by magic, to fix the entity rather than engaging in a description of that entity's relationship to its putative class or classes. In short, 'identity' is a troublesome term, short-circuiting thought and accurate description, and giving a false sense of the mastery of an analytical category over a material reality.

Foucault, too, agrees with Serres, because he prefers not to use the term *identité* when talking about the self. Of course, in the later Foucault, we hear a lot about the self (*soi*), but Foucault also likes to make use of a variety of terms that are cognate with 'subjectivity', such as *sujet*, *assujettir* and *assujettissement*. For example, in *The Use of Pleasure*, Foucault speaks of a 'mode of subjection' (*mode d'assujettissement*) (1986a: 27). Of course, to make some sense of Foucault's choice of language here, it is necessary to understand something of French structuralism and phenomenology. The self is understood as the subject in a linguistic sense (and here Lacan's thought is important) – that is to say, as notionally (grammatically) the one who speaks, but at the same time a function of a social system (language). The subject can simultaneously be the source of action (or the agent), without necessarily being the conscious originator of that action. On the other hand, one can be a subject while simultaneously being 'subjected' – governed by a series of external rules and conventions. Here we also get a hint of the omnipresence of power, in that the subject is both governor and governed, subjecting others while simultaneously him/herself subject to others.

With this kind of subtlety and flexibility, it is unsurprising that Foucault does not favour the prosaic and fixed term *identité*. Yet Foucault is frequently used in 'identity politics' as a justificatory 'great author'. It may be difficult to ground a left or liberatory politics on such an inflexible notion as 'identity' (which is maybe best left to the mathematicians and the logicians); and it seems that there is little use for such a relation in Foucault. Rather, Foucault uses the 'subject' to refer to the various manifestations of self, always-already located within discourses. Just as discourses are plural, so manifestations of subjectivity are plural. Subjectivity is nomadic, temporary, contradictory and heterogeneous, while identity is stable, permanent, coherent and homogeneous. For Foucault, the character of discourse, which he regards as in flux and characterised by martial relationships, does not support something like 'identity'. The subject, the temporary result of specific discursive combinations, is what interests Foucault, yet we can immediately see that the subject represents a kind of 'disempowering' of identity politics: if identity is an illusion, a straitjacket description of something far more tenuous and subtle, if 'the sides' one takes are constantly reformulating and dissolving, then where is the authoritative place from which one can locate the self and be located in order to speak for or against a political position? It is for this reason that one sees in the later Foucault a description of forms of self that seem to be impossible to link to 'politics' in the good old-fashioned sense. In fact, it is possible that Foucault was drawn to scepticism by the dawning realisation of the impossibility of the self being fixed (being identical with anything except itself) and being able to judge (for a fuller discussion of the relationship between Foucault and scepticism, see Kendall and Wickham 1999). However, as Thomas Flynn has pointed out to us, Foucault does allow the contradictory self to act consistently: he likes to use the term *multiplicité* as a way of conveying the idea that a self, though multiple and fractured, can still act in 'singular' fashion. Further, and we are grateful for this point to Mark Bahnisch, a similar observation about the imprecision of 'identity' is made by Jane Flax, although she also stresses how identity has built within it the privileging of the 'default' – the white, middle-class male (see Flax 1998).

Ordering the self

For Foucault then, *soi* is fluid, and tends to escape processes of ordering – it always tends to become 'deterritorialised', as Deleuze and Guattari (e.g. 1988) put it. In contrast, for Latour, the actant is fixed (even as it is 'in process') in the nexus of a network (cf. Michael 1996). Any change is contingent upon other shifts in the network; or rather, there is a jump into another fixed state – another role within a reconfigured network. Where for Foucault there is always the disorder of *soi* lingering beneath the surface of an 'identity', for Latour there are only other potential actant-roles. But, rather than look for disorder as grounded in the essence of the self, we suggest that given that humans (and non-humans, for that matter) are always relational, always between networks, then they are always on the verge of such disorder (and this obviously links up to those moments of innovation captured in the term 'technique').

Bowker and Star (1999) amply illustrate this in their analysis of the many ways in which official classification systems (which are 'technologies' insofar as they are materialised as particular sorts of concrete, movable documents), while reflecting the source network that created them, must also operate in local 'receptor' or 'target' networks. For example, an artefactual non-human transportable system for categorising the causes of death – the International Classification of Diseases (ICD) – will often butt up against local conditions (for example, the workload of physicians, national infrastructures for statistics gathering and processing, and so on) that necessitate innovative practices. The 'implementers' of the ICD thus work around and re-interpret its categories, and innovate in their handling of the documents in which the ICD is partly embodied. In such ways the ICD becomes better 'adjusted' to local conditions. The stable 'singularity' that the ICD 'offers' to the physician (that of 'ICD categoriser of causes of death') is thus 'compromised', or rather, rendered fluid by the sorts of work-arounds and augmentations that make the ICD locally workable semiotically and materially. In other words, new singularities – 'hybrid' or interstitial – emerge. But these new singularities, in turn, become routinised, contingently fixed in the context of local networks. Thus there is a constant oscillation between order and disorder, but we would stress that the tendency to ordering is built in (and here once again what we have in mind is the sort of emphasis upon the inescapability of ordering one sees in the work of Ilya Prigogine and Isabelle Stengers).

Conclusion: network – routine–ordering

Latour enables us to develop a couple of gaps in Foucaultian work, in particular providing us with the means to think seriously about technology (in case we had imagined that Foucault's 'technologies of the self' were enough) and to think seriously about the hybrid character of subjectivity, enabling us to escape from a wrong-headed emphasis on the pure human or the pure social. Latour, then, proposes that our analysis should proceed around the 'network', a loose alliance of actants oriented around certain problems. For Latour, the analytic task comes to be to understand how various actants impose their readings of the world upon others: how they manage to 'interest' certain actants and make sure those actants are not 'interested' in anyone else or any other way of understanding the world (Callon and Latour 1981; Callon and Law 1982). Using Latour as a supplement to Foucault also allows us to see how social orderings and disorderings emerge in the space between instances and systems, or (in the language we have developed for this chapter) between techniques and technologies.

We can spell this out in a shorter form here: networks are the 'problem spaces' around which various actants are organised. The ordering of networks is a constant, but this ordering is always contingent and ongoing. Just like John Law, we prefer the verbal to the substantive form, because 'order' is quite rare, while 'ordering' is ubiquitous. However, networks can become more and more routinised, more and more stable, in which case they *give the appearance* of being more ordered – they become candidates for descriptions using the substantive 'order'. The self (but definitely not 'identity') has an important job to play here, because in its hybrid way it oscillates between fluidity and fixity, between technique and technology, between disorder and order. And we are sure that by now you will know what we urge: describe the appearances of order.

Conclusion: Reshaping Cultural Studies

We have been rather harsh on Cultural Studies throughout this book, but we should stress that our criticisms have been intended to revive and reorient a discipline that we still think can be exciting and innovative. It can also still be political, but it needs to understand politics as only one possible – rather than a necessary – connection that can be made to ordering.

Paul du Gay et al. (1997) have usefully summarised five distinct processes (representation, identity, production, consumption and regulation) that they believe Cultural Studies must focus upon, and it is instructive to take these in turn and see how they fit into Cultural Studies as the study of ordering.

First, representation. Of course, we discussed this issue at some length in Chapter 3 in the context of John Law's work. Representations have typically been of interest in Cultural Studies as a kind of adjunct to ideology theory – that is to say, representations are vital because they are examples of the systematic distortion of reality that is part of the field of culture. John Law's approach is much more sensible, we think, as he is more interested in representations as 'stories' which have effects at a material level (so representations are 'real'). For us, with our emphasis upon a deliberately unprincipled description of appearances, there is no need to treat representations, or stories, as anything special, as we made clear in Chapter 3. All we need do is describe them in the same way we describe all other processes, all other aspects of 'reality'.

Second, identity. As should be clear from Chapter 7, identity is not a concept that helps our reformed Cultural Studies. We are unhappy with its imprecision, and we are unhappy with the way it is linked to a politics of resistance. Our focus has been upon the self (or sometimes the actant), but that self (or actant) must be understood as a component in processes of ordering and disordering. The self cannot be understood as a fixed point outside of networks, but is rather emergent and relational. When we describe processes of ordering, we often end up describing the appearances of self that accompany these processes. We have done this throughout this book, as, for example, in Chapter 4, when we described the appearance of a certain type of ethical personality out of processes of ordering culture through culture.

Third, production. Now, production may refer specifically to an industrial context, but it can also refer more generally to processes of innovation and invention. We have tried to stress in this book that ordering hunts in packs – ordering is linked to a whole series of other ordering projects, and it is the orientation of these projects against and in concert with each other that guarantees novelty. Cultural Studies as the study of ordering will never be too far from a description of the appearances of production, understood more generally, because the dynamism of ordering projects (or networks, as we have occasionally called them) leads inexorably to further ordering projects, which in turn lead to further ordering projects. It does not matter whether the projects succeed or fail (and usually they fail) – they are destined to give birth to further projects. The study of ordering will always incorporate the study of production.

Fourth, consumption. It may seem that consumption is something missing from our new direction for Cultural Studies – and to a certain extent it is, inasmuch as we think consumption (shopping, tourism, restaurant-going, etc.) is an especially important topic for 'late modernity', and we are not concerned to limit our horizons to this historical period. And, of course, in Chapter 6 we spent some time discussing 'consumption activities' as examples of ordering. However, the distinction made in traditional Cultural Studies between production and consumption is informative. Cultural Studies typically differentiates between production (of a physical item, or a media event, or whatever) and its consumption or reception (whether we buy that item, what we make of it, how we understand it and integrate it into our lives). For us, however, such a distinction only encourages the analyst to engage in hermeneutics ('what does this object/event/broadcast really mean?'). Our advice is to set such questions aside – they are unanswerable and spiral infinitely, going nowhere (or, more dangerously, going off to ballast some grand theory or other). More modestly, we follow Harvey Sacks, and Joseph Ford, and Pyrrho of Elis, and Ludwig Wittgenstein, in urging description as the proper limit of inquiry. To this extent, then, we flatten out production and consumption into a single issue and a single methodological request: describe what networks produce, and how those products themselves become integrated into those and other networks.

Fifth, regulation. Of course, to a certain extent this book has been all about regulation. However, we tend to see regulation in a more productive way than has typically been the case in Cultural Studies. That is to say, we understand ordering to be inescapable, and we wish to describe what it makes happen. Some of it will be 'good', and some of it will be 'bad', but the judging is something we leave to you. In fact, we hope you are convinced enough by our arguments that you might even try suspending judgement, although we know just how tough that trick is. But whatever, we wish to move on from the tired old characterisation of regulation as sinister. Everything that we do is 'regulated', or ordered, but without ordering there would be no culture, no innovation, no new possibilities. Of course, you may not think it 'innovative', but, as we discussed earlier, we wrote this book using the 'constraints' imposed upon us by computers, software programmes, an existing Cultural Studies literature, and so forth. If you prefer to think through other, more clearly 'creative' examples, 'regulation' is ubiquitous. Stephen Jay Gould (1998), for example, presents a striking analysis of how elements of the Mona Lisa owe their existence to the 'constraints' of da Vinci's theories about the how the world and the human body work by analogous principles. Our point here is that the Mona Lisa is, of course, a great and 'innovative' work of art – but 'regulation', or better, ordering, is the *sine qua non* of its existence.

Now it still seems to us that Cultural Studies is enormously important. Not least of its contributions has been its ability to focus on issues that have previously seemed beneath the dignity of the scholar. Cultural Studies has turned our attention to all kinds of new objects and processes, and to the extent that it has inherited and extended the noble tradition of writers like Marcel Mauss and Norbert Elias, directing our attention to the miscellany of everyday life, we salute it. We are far from wishing to join the sorts of attacks on Cultural Studies which impugn its subject matter and question whether it is a real discipline (as Bourdieu and Wacquant 1999, for example, have done recently). But it needs to be strengthened, and we close by reiterating two points we made in Chapter 1. First, we agree with Tony Bennett (1998) in calling for Cultural Studies to develop a pragmatics, to admit that it is a discipline. In a sense, Bennett is telling Cultural Studies to grow up and accept a more mature role for itself. It must give up being 'speculative', as McHoul and Miller (1998) rightly point out, and accept that a new rigour in terms of its objects of study and its methodology need not be *rigor mortis*. Second, it must give up its obsession with power and meaning. We have suggested some alternative obsessions for Culture Studies – with ordering and with description – that we think will serve it better in the years ahead. We do not think this constitutes a 'selling out' of Cultural Studies – indeed if its practitioners still wish to use the discipline as a way to analyse politics and power, they may find (and we sincerely hope) that they can do so from a stronger footing.

References

Alexander, J.C. and Seidman, S. (eds) (1990) *Culture and Society: Contemporary Debates*. Cambridge: Cambridge University Press.

Alldridge, P. (1993) '"Attempted murder of the soul": blackmail, privacy and secrets', *Oxford Journal of Legal Studies* 13(3): 368–87.

Annas, J. and Barnes, J. (1994) 'Introduction'. In Sextus Empiricus, *Outlines of Scepticism* (translated by J. Annas and J. Barnes). Cambridge: Cambridge University Press.

Anon (1861) *On Some Features of Colonial Life: A Lecture Delivered at Queenscliffe on the 15th February 1861*. Melbourne.

Arnold, M. (1932) [1869] *Culture and Anarchy*. Cambridge: Cambridge University Press.

Barry, A., Osborne, T. and Rose, N. (eds) (1996) *Foucault and Political Reason: Liberalism, Neo-Liberalism and Rationalities of Government*. London: UCL Press.

Bauman, Z. (1989) *Modernity and the Holocaust*. Cambridge: Polity.

Beaglehole, J.C. (1967) 'The Colonial Office 1782–1854'. In M. Beever and F.B. Smith (eds), *Historical Studies: Selected Articles Second Series*. Melbourne: Melbourne University Press.

Bennett, T. (1992) 'Putting policy into cultural studies'. In L. Grossberg, C. Nelson and P. Treichler (eds), *Cultural Studies*. London: Routledge.

Bennett, T. (1998) *Culture: A Reformer's Science*. St Leonards: Allen & Unwin.

Berger, A.A. (ed.) (1998) *The Postmodern Presence: Readings on Postmodernism in American Culture and Society*. Walnut Creek, CA: AltaMira Press.

Boas, F. (1920) 'The methods of ethnology', *American Anthropologist* 22: 311–21.

Boas, F. (1938) *The Mind of Primitive Man*. New York: Macmillan.

Borkowski, A. (1994) *Textbook on Roman Law*. London: Butterworths.

Bourdieu, P. and Wacquant, L. (1999) 'The new global vulgate', *The Baffler* 12: 69–78.

Bowker, G. and Star, S.L. (1999) *Sorting Things Out: Classification and Its Consequences*. Cambridge, MA: MIT Press.

Brigham, J. (1999) 'The Constitution of the Supreme Court'. In H. Gillman and C. Clayton (eds), *The Supreme Court and American Politics*. Lawrence: University of Kansas Press.

Brown, D., Neal, D., Farrier, D. and Weisbrot, D. (1990) *Criminal Laws*. Sydney: Federation Press.

Brown, P. (1988) *The Body and Society: Men, Women, and Sexual Renunciation in Early Christianity*. New York: Columbia University Press.

Bryce, Viscount James (1914) *The Ancient Roman Empire and the British Empire in India: The Diffusion of Roman and English Law throughout the World, etc.* London: Oxford University Press.

Bryson, B. (1994) *Made in America: An Informal History of the English Language in the United States*. New York: William Morrow & Co.

Buck-Morss, S. (1986) 'The flâneur, the sandwichman and the whore: the politics of loitering', *New German Critique* 39: 99–140.

Buller, C. (1840) *Responsible Government for Colonies*. London (published anonymously).

Burke, Sir (John) Bernard (1884) *The General Armory of England, Scotland, Ireland, and Wales: Comprising a Registry of Armorial Bearings from the Earliest to the Present Time*. London: Harrison & Sons.

Burke, Sir (John) Bernard (1891) *A Genealogical and Heraldic History of the Colonial Gentry*, Volume 1. London: Harrison & Sons.

Burke, Sir (John) Bernard (1895) *A Genealogical and Heraldic History of the Colonial Gentry*, Volume 2. London: Harrison & Sons.

Callon, M. (1986) 'Some elements of a sociology of translation: domestication of the scallops and the fishermen of St Brieuc Bay'. In J. Law (ed.), *Power, Action and Belief: A New Sociology of Knowledge?* London: Routledge & Kegan Paul.

Callon, M. and Latour, B. (1981) 'Unscrewing the big Leviathan: how actors macro-structure reality and how sociologists help them to do so'. In K. Knorr-Cetina and A. Cicourel (eds), *Advances in Social Theory and Methodology*. London: Routledge & Kegan Paul.

Callon, M. and Law, J. (1982) 'On interests and their transformation: enrolment and counter-enrolment', *Social Studies of Science* 12, 615–25.

Collins, H.M. and Yearley, S. (1992) 'Epistemological chicken'. In A. Pickering (ed.), *Science as Practice and Culture*. Chicago: Chicago University Press.

Collins, R. and Makowsky, M. (1998) *The Discovery of Society* (sixth edition). Boston: McGraw-Hill.

Cooper, G. (1997) 'Textual technologies: new literary forms and reflexivity'. In J. Collier with D. Twomey (eds), *Scientific and Technical Communication: Theory, Practice, and Policy*. London: Sage.

Crane, D. (1995) 'Introduction: Culture syllabi and the sociology of culture: what do syllabi tell us?' In D. Crane and M.S. Larson (eds), *Course Syllabi for the Sociology of Culture*. Washington, DC: American Sociological Association.

Curnow, G.R. (1975) 'Professionals in bureaucracies'. In R.N. Spann and G.R. Curnow (eds), *Public Policy and Administration in Australia: A Reader*. Sydney: Hale & Iremonger.

Davidson, A. (1991) *The Invisible State: The Formation of the Australian State 1788–1901*. Cambridge: Cambridge University Press.

Dean, M. (1999) *Governmentality*. London: Sage.

de Certeau, M. (1984) *The Practice of Everyday Life*. Berkeley: University of California Press.

Deleuze, G. and Guattari, F. (1988) *A Thousand Plateaus: Capitalism and Schizophrenia*. London: Athlone Press.

de Serville, P. (1980) *Port Phillip Gentlemen and Good Society in Melbourne before the Gold Rushes*. Melbourne: Oxford University Press.

de Serville, P. (1991) *Pounds and Pedigrees: The Upper Class in Victoria 1850–80*. Melbourne: Oxford University Press.

du Gay, P., Hall, S., Janes, L., Mackay, H. and Negus, K. (1997) *Doing Cultural Studies: The Story of the Sony Walkman*. London: Sage.

Elias, N. (1978) *The Civilizing Process*, Vol. 1: *The History of Manners*. Oxford: Blackwell.

Ericson, R. and Haggerty, K. (1997) *Policing the Risk Society*. Toronto: University of Toronto Press.

Ewick, P. and Silbey, S. (1992) 'Conformity, contestation, and resistance: an account of legal consciousness', *New England Law Review* 26(3): 731–49.

Ewick, P. and Silbey, S. (1995) 'Subversive stories and hegemonic tales: towards a sociology of narrative', *Law and Society Review* 29(2): 197–226.

Fishman, M. and Cavender, G. (eds) (1998) *Entertaining Crime: Television Reality Programs*. New York: Aldine de Gruyter.

Fiske, J. (1986) 'British cultural studies and television'. In R.C. Allen (ed.), *Channels of Discourse*. Chapel Hill: University of North Carolina Press.

Fiske, J. and Hartley, J. (1978) *Reading Television*. London: Methuen.

Flaschka, H. and Chirikov, B. (eds) (1988) *Progress in Chaotic Dynamics: Essays in Honor of Joseph Ford's 60th Birthday*. Amsterdam: Elsevier.

Flax, J. (1998) 'Displacing woman: toward an ethics of multiplicity'. In B.-A. Bar On and A. Ferguson (eds), *Daring to be Good: Essays in Feminist Ethico-Politics*. New York: Routledge.

Foucault, M. (1970) *The Order of Things: An Archaeology of the Human Sciences*. London: Tavistock.

Foucault, M. (1977) *Discipline and Punish: The Birth of the Prison*. London: Allen Lane.

Foucault, M. (1978) *The History of Sexuality*, Vol. 1: *An Introduction*. New York: Pantheon.

Foucault, M. (1986a) *The Use of Pleasure*. London: Viking.

Foucault, M. (1986b) *The Care of the Self*. New York: Pantheon.

Foucault, M. (1991) 'Governmentality'. In G. Burchell, C. Gordon and P. Miller (eds), *The Foucault Effect: Studies in Governmentality*. Hemel Hempstead: Harvester Wheatsheaf.

Frazer, J. G. (1890) *The Golden Bough: A Study in Magic and Religion*. London: Macmillan.

Frith, S. (1988) *Music for Pleasure: Essays in the Sociology of Pop*. Cambridge: Polity.

Frow, J. (1991) 'Michel de Certeau and the practice of representation', *Cultural Studies* 5(1): 52–60.

Frow, J. and Morris, M. (1993) *Australian Cultural Studies: A Reader*. St Leonards: Allen & Unwin.

Gane, M. (ed.) (1986) *Towards a Critique of Foucault*. London: Routledge & Kegan Paul.

Geertz, C. (1991) 'Deep play: the Balinese cockfight'. In C. Mukerji and M. Schudson (eds), *Rethinking Popular Culture: Contemporary Perspectives in Cultural Studies*. Berkeley: University of California Press.

Geertz, C. (2000) *Local Knowledge: Further Essays in Interpretive Anthropology.* New York: Basic Books.

Gellner, E. (1998) *Language and Solitude: Wittgenstein, Malinowski and the Habsburg Dilemma.* Cambridge: Cambridge University Press.

Gillies, J. (1792) *The History of Ancient Greece*, 2 vols. London: A. Strahan and T. Cadell.

Gould, S.J. (1989) *Wonderful Life: The Burgess Shale and the Nature of History.* New York: W.W. Norton & Company.

Gould, S.J. (1991) 'The streak of streaks' in *Bully for Brontosaurus: Reflections on Natural History.* London: Hutchinson.

Gould, S.J. (1998) *Leonardo's Mountain of Clams and the Diet of Worms: Essays on Natural History.* London: Jonathan Cape.

Gowan, P. (1987) 'The origins of the administrative elite', *New Left Review* 162, 4–34.

Gramsci, A. (1978) *Selections from the Prison Notebooks.* New York: International.

Great Britain and Ireland – Colonial Office (1843) *Rules and Regulations for Her Majesty's Colonial Service.* London: HMSO.

Grossberg, L., Wartella, E. and Whitney, D.C. (1998) *Mediamaking: Mass Media in a Popular Culture.* Thousand Oaks, CA: Sage.

Grote, G. (1869) *A History of Greece.* London: John Murray.

Hadot, P. (1995) *Philosophy as a Way of Life: Spiritual Exercises from Socrates to Foucault.* Oxford: Blackwell.

Hall, S. (1980) 'Cultural Studies: two paradigms', *Media, Culture and Society* 2: 57–72.

Hall, S. (1992) 'Cultural Studies and its theoretical legacies'. In L. Grossberg, C. Nelson and P. Treichler (eds), *Cultural Studies.* London: Routledge.

Hall, S. and Jefferson, T. (eds) (1976) *Resistance through Rituals: Youth Subcultures in Post-War Britain.* London: Hutchinson.

Hankinson, R.J. (1995) *The Sceptics.* London: Routledge.

Haraway, D. (1991) *Simians, Cyborgs and Women.* London: Routledge.

Hartley, J. (1999) *Uses of Television.* London: Routledge.

Hay, D. (1975) 'Property, authority and the criminal law' in D. Hay et al., *Albion's Fatal Tree: Crime and Society in Eighteenth-Century England.* London: Allen Lane.

Hayward, P. (ed.) (1992) *From Pop to Punk to Postmodernism: Popular Music and Australian Culture from the 1960s to the 1990s.* North Sydney: Allen & Unwin.

Hebdige, D. (1979) *Subculture: The Meaning of Style.* London: Methuen.

Hirst, J.B. (1988) *The Strange Birth of Colonial Democracy: New South Wales 1848–1884.* Sydney: Allen & Unwin.

Hirst, P. and Woolley, P. (1982) *Social Relations and Human Attributes.* London: Tavistock.

Hogan, M. (1988) 'Police use of deadly force: when is it right to pull the trigger?' In M. Hogan, D. Brown and R. Hogg (eds), *Death in the Hands of the State.* Sydney: Redfern Legal Centre Press.

Hogg, R. (1987) 'The politics of criminal investigation'. In G. Wickham (ed.), *Social Theory and Legal Politics.* Sydney: Local Consumption Publications.

Hogg, R. (1988) 'Police "hot" pursuits: the need for restraint'. In M. Hogan, D.

Brown and R. Hogg (eds), *Death in the Hands of the State*. Sydney: Redfern Legal Centre Press.

Hoggart, R. (1957) *The Uses of Literacy*. Oxford: Oxford University Press.

Hunt, A. and Wickham, G. (1994) *Foucault and Law: Towards a Sociology of Law as Governance*. London: Pluto.

Hunter, I. (1988) *Culture and Government: The Emergence of Literary Education*. London: Macmillan.

Hunter, I. (1992) 'Aesthetics and Cultural Studies'. In L. Grossberg, C. Nelson and P. Treichler (eds), *Cultural Studies*. London: Routledge.

Hunter, I. (1994) *Rethinking the School: Subjectivity, Bureaucracy, Criticism*. Sydney: Allen & Unwin.

Huskisson, W. (1831) *The Speeches of the Right Hon. W. Huskisson, with a Biographical Memoir*, 3 Vols. London.

Jenkyns, R. (1980) *The Victorians and Ancient Greece*. Oxford: Blackwell.

Kellner, D. (1995) *Media Culture: Cultural Studies, Identity, and Politics Between the Modern and the Postmodern*. London: Routledge.

Kendall, G. (1997) 'Governing at a distance: Anglo-Australian relations 1840–1870', *Australian Journal of Political Science* 32(2): 223–35.

Kendall, G. (1999) 'Pop music: authenticity, creativity, technology', *Social Alternatives* 18(2): 24–8.

Kendall, G. and Michael, M. (1998) 'Thinking the unthought: towards a Moebius Strip psychology', *New Ideas in Psychology* 16(3): 141–57.

Kendall, G. and Wickham, G. (1996) 'Governing the culture of cities: a Foucaultian framework', *Southern Review* 29(2): 202–19.

Kendall, G. and Wickham, G. (1999) *Using Foucault's Methods*. London: Sage.

Knox, B. (1992) 'Democracy, aristocracy and empire: the provision of colonial honours, 1818–1870', *Australian Historical Studies* 99: 244–64.

Kociumbas, J. (1992) *The Oxford History of Australia*, Vol. 2, *1770–1860: Possessions*. Oxford: Oxford University Press.

Kuklick, H. (1991) *The Savage Within*. Cambridge: Cambridge University Press.

Lang, J.D. (1852) *Freedom and Independence for the Golden Lands of Australia*. London: Longman & Co.

Lang, J.D. (1854) *An Anatomical Lecture on the New Constitution*. Sydney: F. Cunninghame.

Larner, C. (1981) *Enemies of God: The Witch-Hunt in Scotland*. London: Chatto & Windus.

Latour, B. (1986) 'The powers of association'. In J. Law (ed.), *Power, Belief and Action*. London: Routledge.

Latour, B. (1987) *Science in Action: How to Follow Engineers in Society*. Milton Keynes: Open University Press.

Latour, B. (1990) 'Drawing things together'. In M. Lynch and S. Woolgar (eds), *Representation in Scientific Practice*. London: MIT Press.

Latour, B. (1992) 'Where are the missing masses?' In W. Bijker and J. Law (eds), *Shaping Technology/Building Society*. Cambridge, MA: MIT Press.

Latour, B. (1993) *We Have Never Been Modern*. Hemel Hempstead: Harvester Wheatsheaf.

Latour, B. (1999) *Pandora's Hope: Essays on the Reality of Science Studies*. Cambridge, MA: Harvard University Press.

Law, J. (1986) 'On the methods of long-distance control: vessels, navigation and the Portuguese route to India'. In J. Law (ed.), *Power, Belief and Action*. London: Routledge.

Law, J. (1994) *Organizing Modernity*. Oxford: Blackwell.

Livingstone, R.W. (1912) *The Greek Genius and its Meaning to Us*. Oxford: Clarendon.

Loveday, P. (1959) 'Patronage and politics in NSW, 1856–1870', *Public Administration (Sydney)* 18(4): 341–58.

Lucas, C.P. (1912) *Greater Rome and Greater Britain*. Oxford: Clarendon.

McHoul, A. and Miller, T. (1998) *Popular Culture and Everyday Life*. London: Sage.

Macintyre, S. (1991) *A Colonial Liberalism: The Lost World of Three Victorian Visionaries*. Melbourne: Oxford.

McKinley, E.G. (1997) *Beverly Hills, 90210: Television, Gender, and Identity*. Philadelphia : University of Pennsylvania Press.

McMartin, A. (1959) 'Aspects of patronage in Australia 1786–1836', *Public Administration (Sydney)* 18(4): 326–40.

Maconochie, Capt. A. (1839) *Australiana: Thoughts on Convict Management and Other Subjects Connected with the Australian Penal Colonies*. London: John W. Parker.

Malinowski, B. (1926) *Crime and Custom in Savage Society*. New York: Harcourt, Brace & Co.

Malinowski, B. (1984) [1948] *Magic, Science, and Religion, and Other Essays*. Westport, CT: Greenwood Press.

Malpas, J. and Wickham, G. (1995) 'Governance and failure: on the limits of sociology', *Australian and New Zealand Journal of Sociology* 31(3): 37–50.

Malpas, J. and Wickham, G. (1997) 'Governance and the world: from Joe DiMaggio to Michel Foucault', *The UTS Review* 3(2): 91–108.

Martin, L.H., Gutman, H. and Hutton, P.H. (eds) (1988) *Technologies of the Self: A Seminar with Michel Foucault*. Amherst: University of Massachusetts Press.

Mauss, M. (1973) 'Techniques of the body', *Economy and Society* 2(1): 70–88.

Mead, M. (1964) *Continuities in Cultural Evolution*. New Haven, CT: Yale University Press.

Mead, M. (1976) [1937] *Co-operation and Competition among Primitive Peoples*. Gloucester, MA: P. Smith.

Merivale, H. (1861) *Lectures on Colonization and Colonies*. London: Longman, Green, Longman, & Roberts.

Michael, M. (1996) *Constructing Identities: The Social, the Nonhuman and Change*. London: Sage.

Michael, M. (2000) *Reconnecting Culture, Technology and Nature: From Society to Heterogeneity*. London: Routledge.

Miller, P. (1992) 'Accounting and objectivity: the invention of calculating selves and calculable spaces', *Annals of Scholarship* 9(2): 61–86.

Miller, T. (1992) *The Well-Tempered Self: Citizenship, Culture, and the Postmodern Subject*. Baltimore, MD: Johns Hopkins University Press.

Morgan, L.H. (1877) *Ancient Society: Or, Researches in the Lines of Human Progress from Savagery through Barbarism to Civilization*. Chicago: Charles H. Kerr.

Morgan, L.H. (1997) [1876] *Systems of Consanguinity and Affinity of the Human Family*. Lincoln: University of Nebraska Press.

Morley, D. (1992) *Television, Audiences and Cultural Studies*. London: Routledge.

Morrell, W.P. (1966) [1930] *British Colonial Policy in the Age of Peel and Russell*. London: Cass.

Morris, M. (1990) 'Banality in Cultural Studies'. In P. Mellencamp (ed.), *Logics of Television: Essays in Cultural Criticism*. Bloomington: Indiana University Press.

Mukerji, C. and Schudson, M. (eds) (1991) *Rethinking Popular Culture: Contemporary Perspectives in Cultural Studies*. Berkeley: University of California Press.

Nietzsche, F.W. (1918) *The Genealogy of Morals*. New York: Boni and Liveright.

Ogilvie, R.M. (1964) *Latin and Greek: A History of the Influence of the Classics on English Life from 1600 to 1918*. London: Routledge & Kegan Paul.

O'Malley, P. (1983) *Law, Capitalism and Democracy*. Sydney: Allen & Unwin.

O'Malley, P. (1998–9) 'Imagining insurance: risk, thrift and industrial life insurance in Britain', *Connecticut Insurance Law Journal* 5(2): 676–705.

O'Malley, P. (1999) 'Governmentality and the risk society', *Economy and Society* 28(1): 138–48.

Osborne, T. (1994) 'Bureaucracy as a vocation: governmentality and administration in nineteenth-century Britain', *Journal of Historical Sociology* 7(3): 289–313.

Osborne, T. (1998) *Aspects of Enlightenment: Social Theory and the Ethics of Truth*. London: University of London Press.

Parker, R.S. (1989) 'The quest for administrative leadership', *Political Science* 41(2): 18–29.

Perec, G. (1997) *Species of Space and Other Pieces*. London: Penguin.

Peters, E. (1985) *Torture*. Oxford: Blackwell.

Pitt Rivers, W.H. (1922) *History and Ethnology*. New York: Macmillan.

Pitt Rivers, W.H. (1934) 'Primitive man'. In E. Eyre (ed.), *European Civilization*. Oxford: Oxford University Press.

Pitt Rivers, W.H. (1939) *The Culture Historical Method of Ethnology*. New York: Fortuny's.

Prigogine, I. and Stengers, I. (1984) *Order out of Chaos: Man's New Dialogue with Nature*. New York: Bantam Books.

Prigogine, I. and Stengers, I. (1997) *The End of Certainty: Time, Chaos, and the New Laws of Nature*. New York: Free Press.

Pue, W.W. (1997) 'Lawyers and political Liberalism in eighteenth- and nineteenth-century England'. In T.C. Halliday and L. Karpik (eds), *Lawyers and the Rise of Western Political Liberalism: Europe and North America from the Eighteenth to Twentieth Centuries*. Oxford: Clarendon.

Roe, M. (1965) *Quest for Authority in Eastern Australia 1835–1851*. Melbourne: Melbourne University Press.

Rose, N. (1990) *Governing the Soul: The Shaping of the Private Self*. London: Routledge.

Rose, N. (1999) *Powers of Freedom: Reframing Political Thought*. Cambridge: Cambridge University Press.

Rose, N. and Miller, P. (1992) 'Political power beyond the state: problematics of government', *British Journal of Sociology* 43(2): 173–205.

Rothblatt, S. (1976) *Tradition and Change in English Liberal Education*. London: Faber.

Said, E. (1978) *Orientalism*. Harmondsworth: Penguin.

Seeley, Sir John Robert (1883) *The Expansion of England: Two Courses of Lectures*. London: Macmillan & Co.

Serres, M. (1998) 'Unpublished seminar'. University of Queensland, Brisbane, Australia, October.

Sextus Empiricus (1994) *Outlines of Scepticism* (translated by J. Annas and J. Barnes). Cambridge: Cambridge University Press.

Silverman, D. (1998) *Harvey Sacks: Conversation Analysis and Social Science*. Cambridge: Polity.

Smith, G.E. (1928) *In the Beginning: The Origin of Civilization*. New York: Morrow.

Smith, G.E. (1931) 'The influence of ancient Egyptian civilization in the East and in America'. In V.F. Calverton (ed.), *The Making of Man: An Outline of Anthropology*. New York: Modern Library.

Smith, G.E. (1933) *The Diffusion of Culture*. London: Watts.

Stephens, W. (1895) *The Life and Letters of Edward A. Freeman*. London.

Stocking, G. (1982) *Race, Culture and Evolution*. London: University of Chicago Press.

Stocking, G. (1992) *The Ethnographer's Magic*. London: University of Wisconsin Press.

The Unknown (1865) *Prospects and Considerations of a Future for the Australian Colonies: A Pamphlet*. Hobart: J. Walch and Sons.

Thompson, E.P. (1968) *The Making of the English Working Class*. Harmondsworth: Penguin.

Toulmin, S. (1994) 'Foreword'. In J.E. Malpas (ed.), *The Philosophical Papers of Alan Donagan*, Vol. 1: *Historical Understanding and the History of Philosophy*. Chicago: University of Chicago Press.

Turner, F.M. (1981) *The Greek Heritage in Victorian Britain*. New Haven, CT: Yale University Press.

Tylor, E.B. (1871) *Primitive Culture: Researches into the Development of Mythology, Philosophy, Religion, Language, Art and Custom*. New York: H. Holt.

van Caenegem, R.C. (1991) 'Criminal law in England and Flanders under King Henry II and Count Philip of Alsace'. In R.C. van Caenegem, *Legal History: A European Perspective*. London: Hambledon Press.

Veyne, P. (1992) 'Introduction' and 'The Roman Empire'. In P. Veyne (ed.), *The History of Private Life*, Vol. 1: *From Pagan Rome to Byzantium*. Cambridge, MA: Harvard University Press.

Wakefield, E.G. (1914) [1849] *A View of the Art of Colonization*. Oxford: J. Collier.

Weber, M. (1989) [1930] *The Protestant Ethic and the Spirit of Capitalism*. London: Unwin Hyman.

Williams, R. (1958) *Culture and Society, 1780–1950*. New York: Columbia University Press.

Williams, R. (1961) *The Long Revolution*. Penguin: Harmondsworth.

Williams, R. (1974) *Television, Technology, and Cultural Form*. London: Fontana.

Williams, R. (1976) *Keywords: A Vocabulary of Culture and Society*. London: Fontana.

Williams, R. (1983) *Keywords: A Vocabulary of Culture and Society* (Second edition). London: Fontana.

Wittgenstein, L. (1979) *On Certainty*. Oxford: Blackwell.

Wright, J. (1847) *Outline of a Plan for a General and Continuous Colonization Society*. London: C. Dolman.

Index